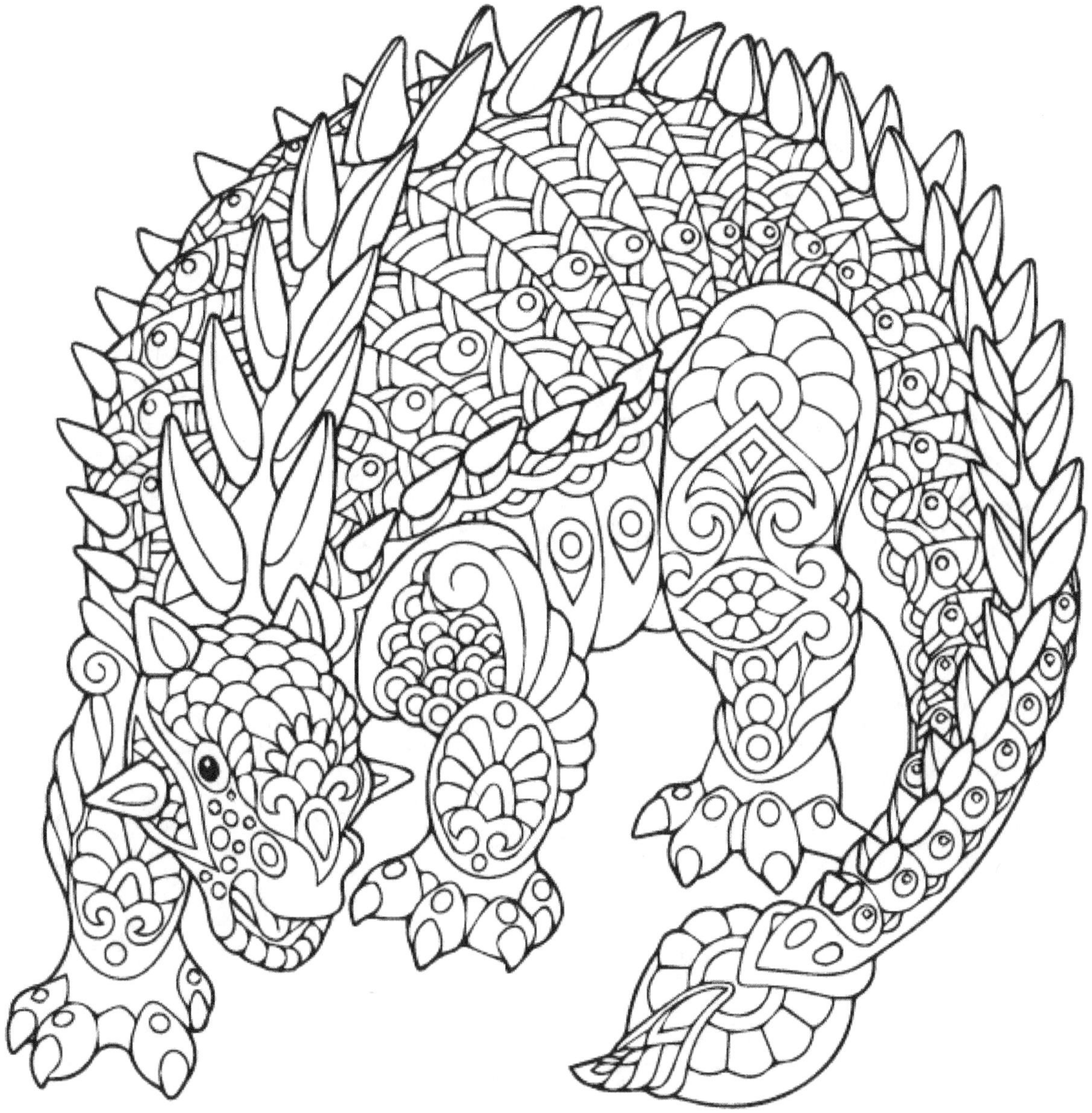

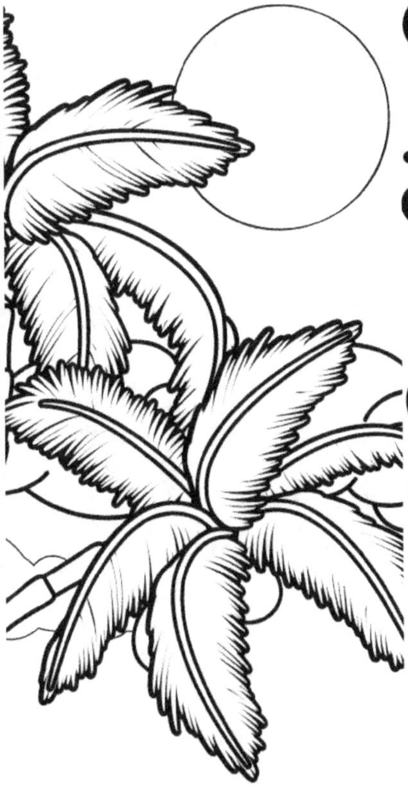

THIS BOOK
BELONGS TO...

....

....

....

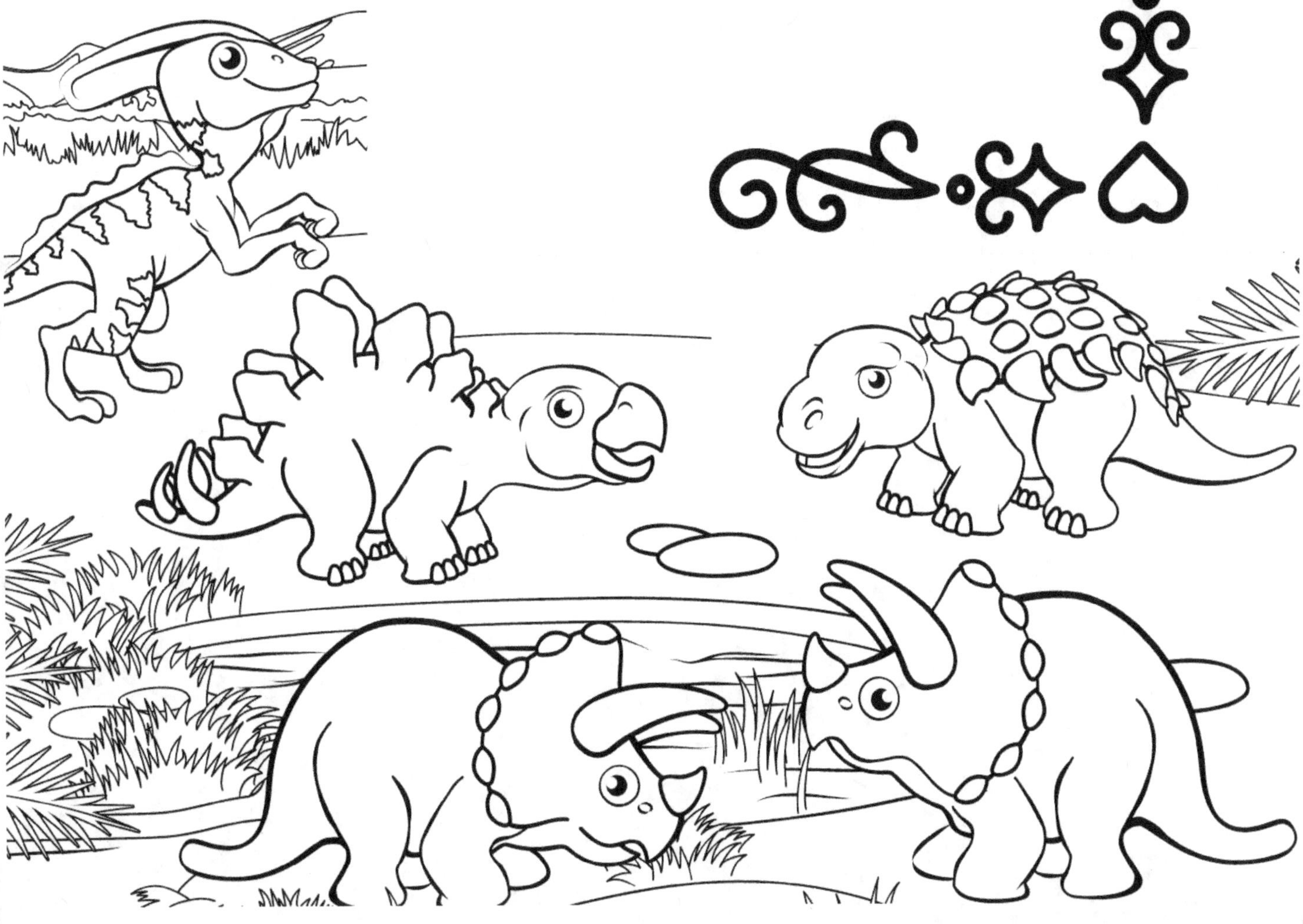

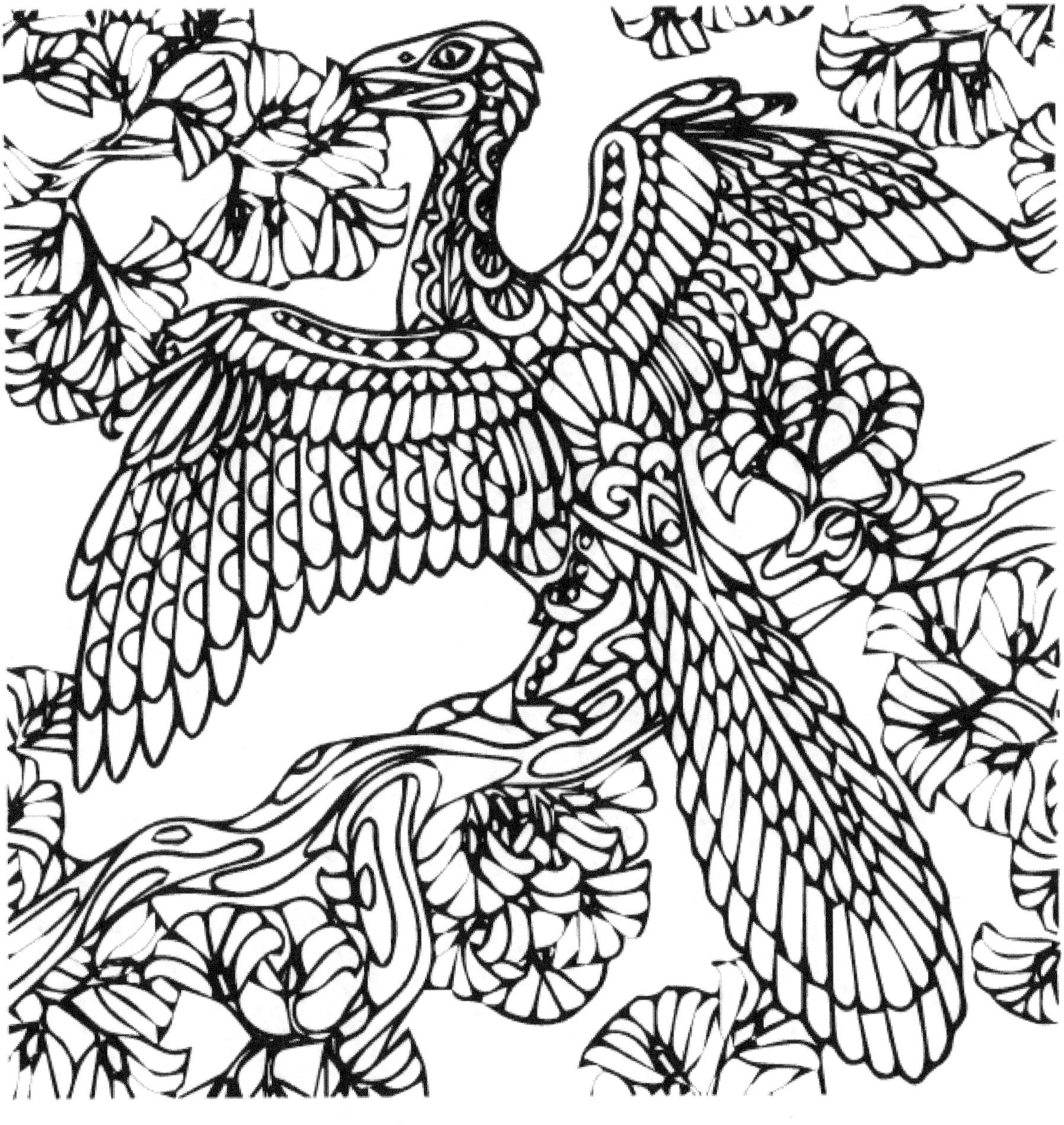

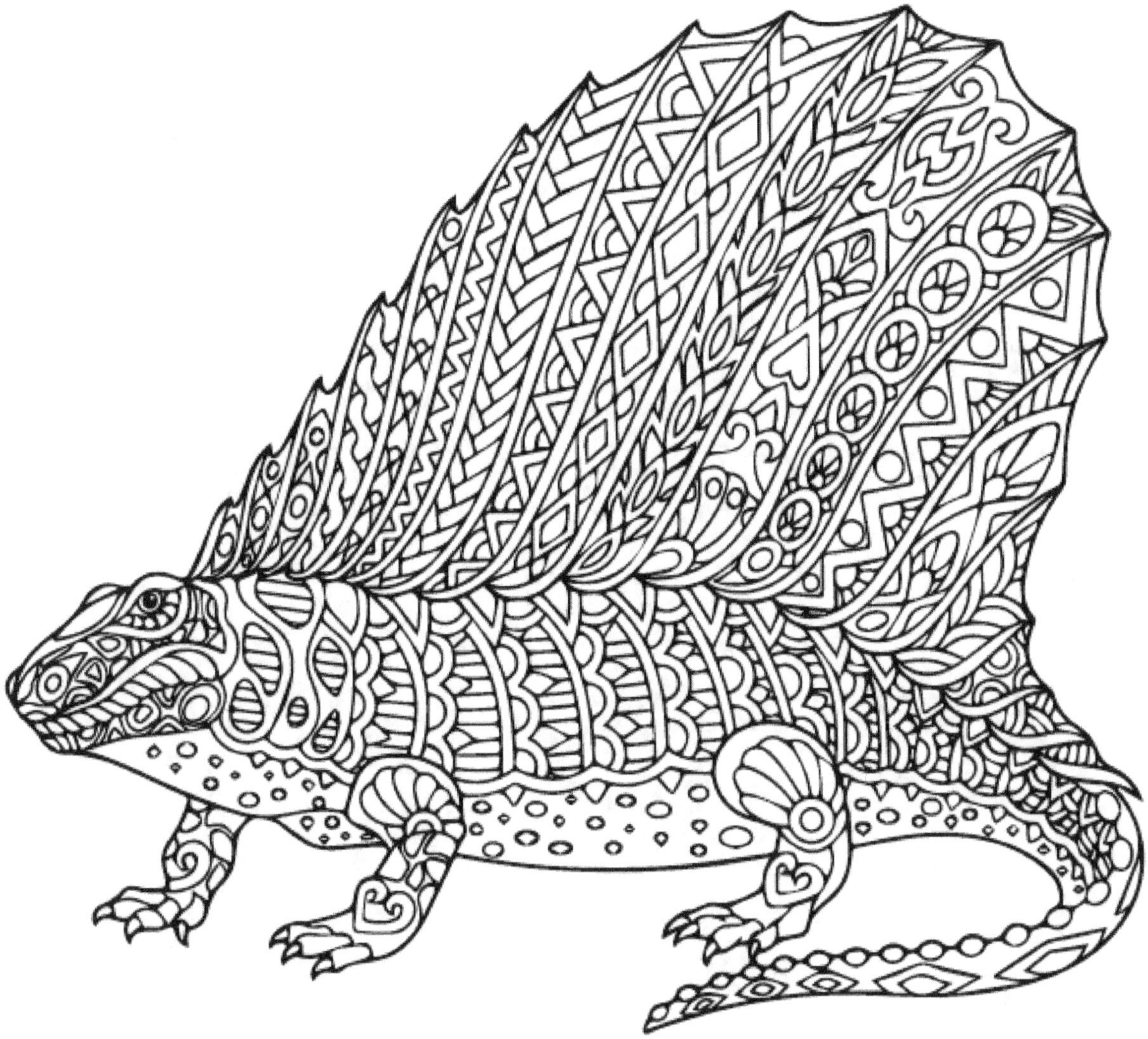

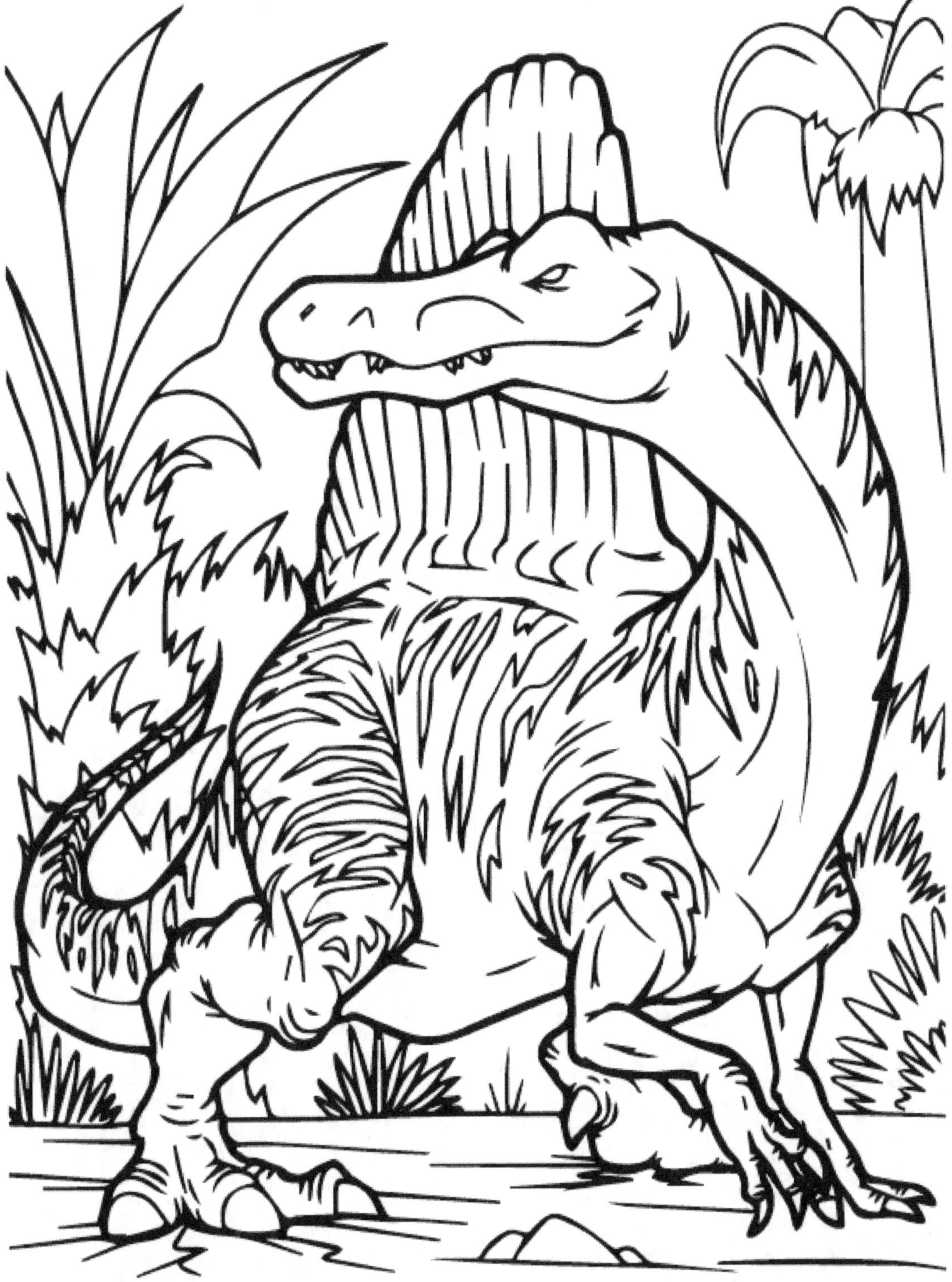

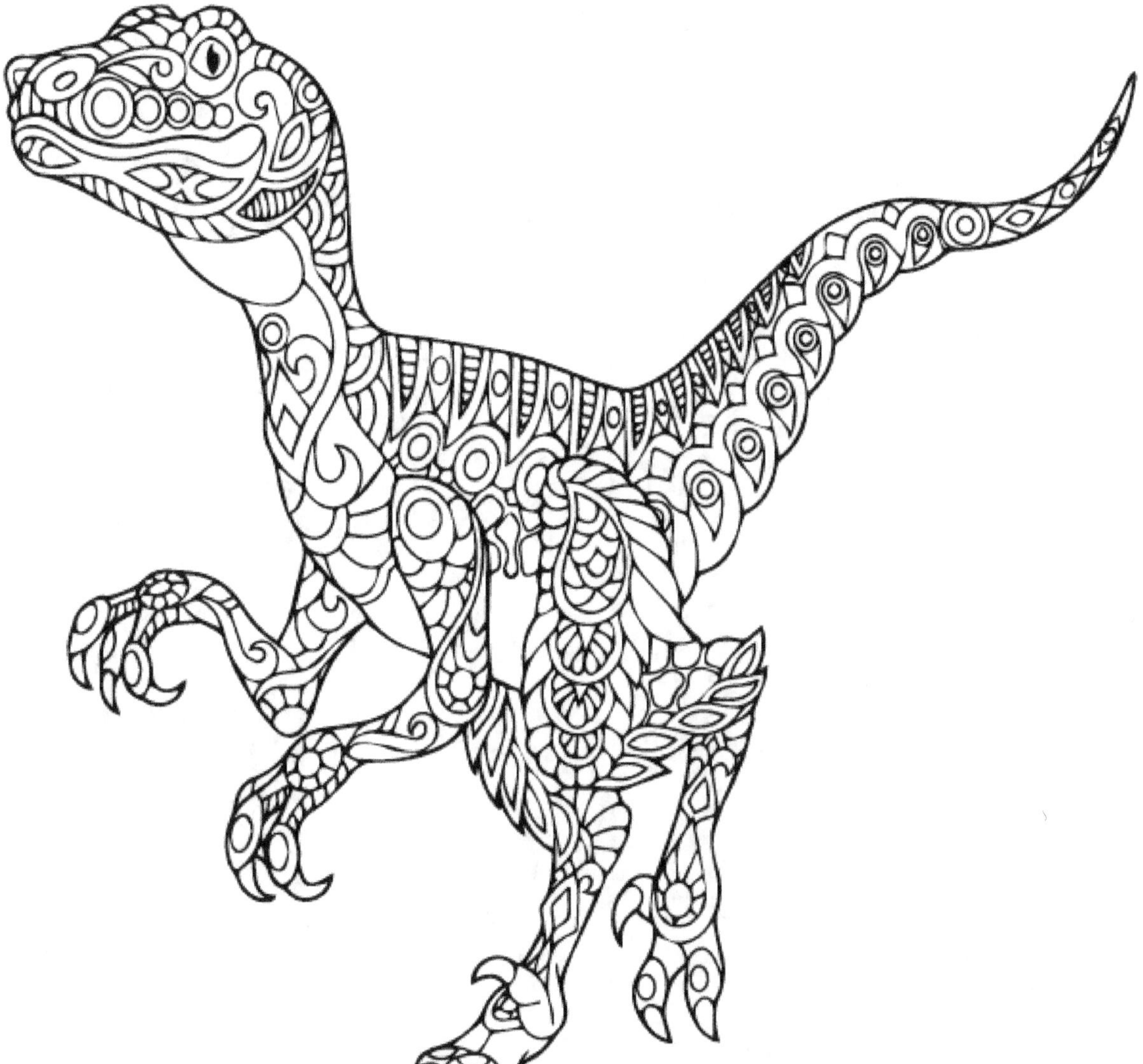

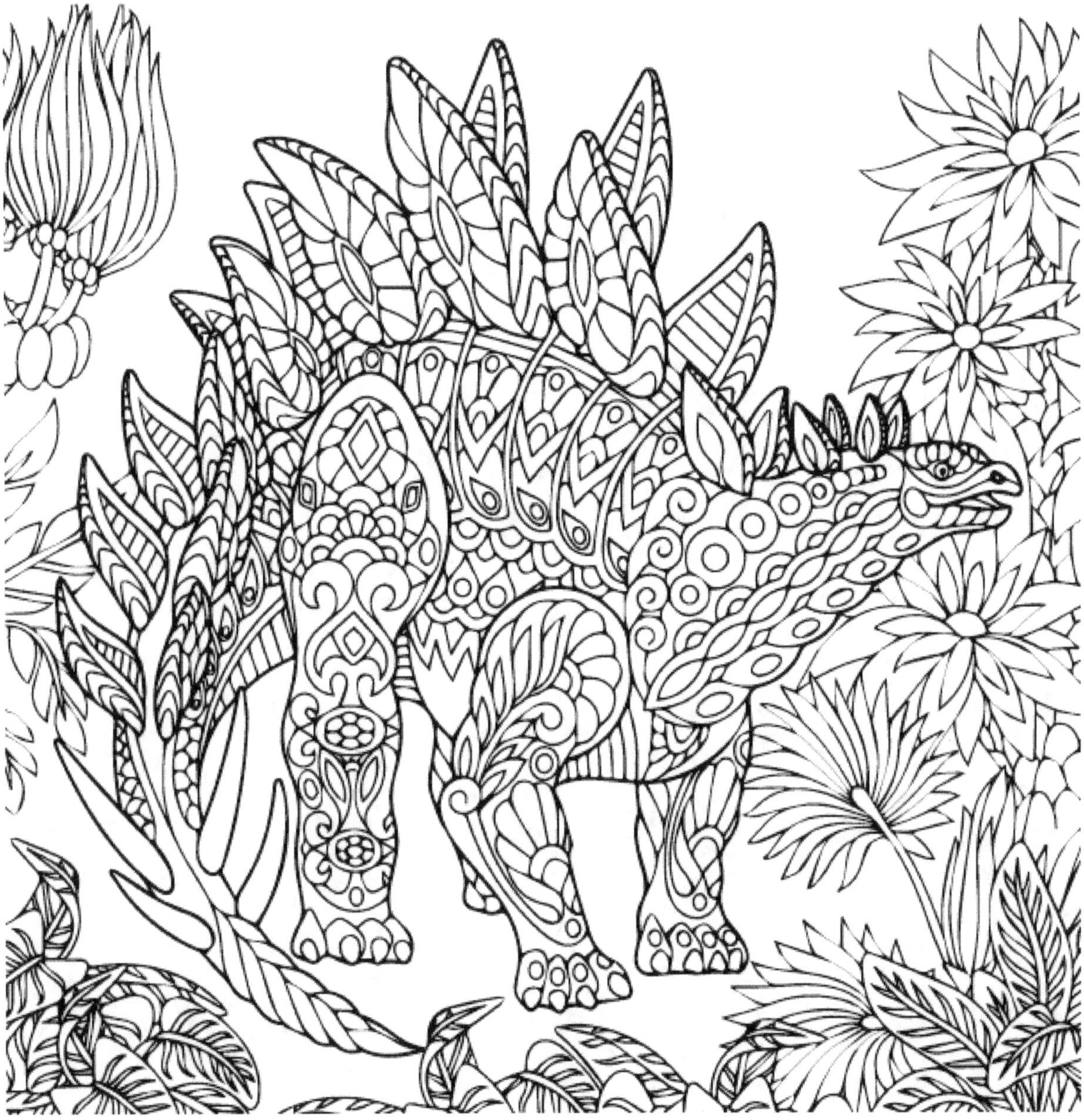

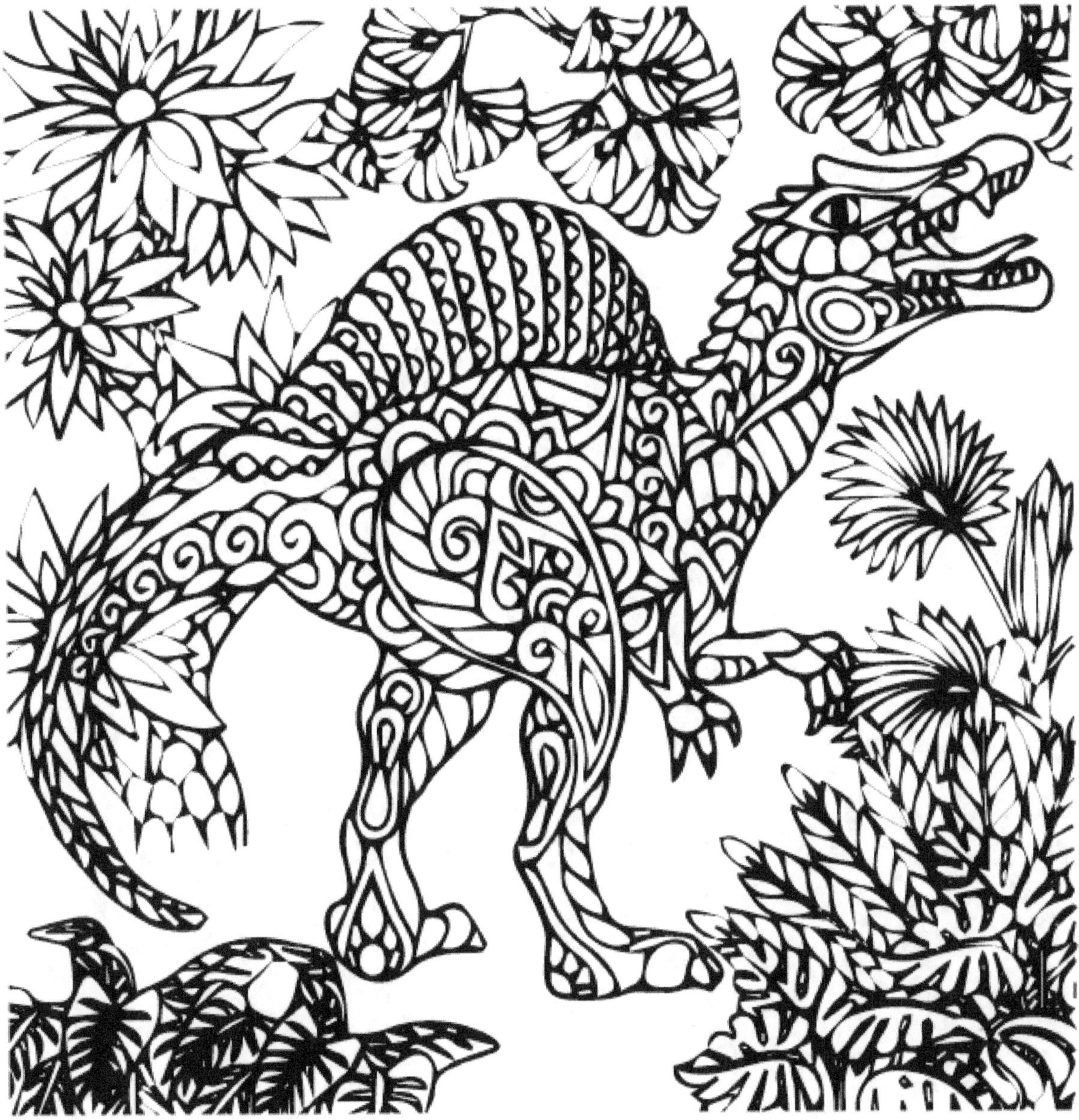

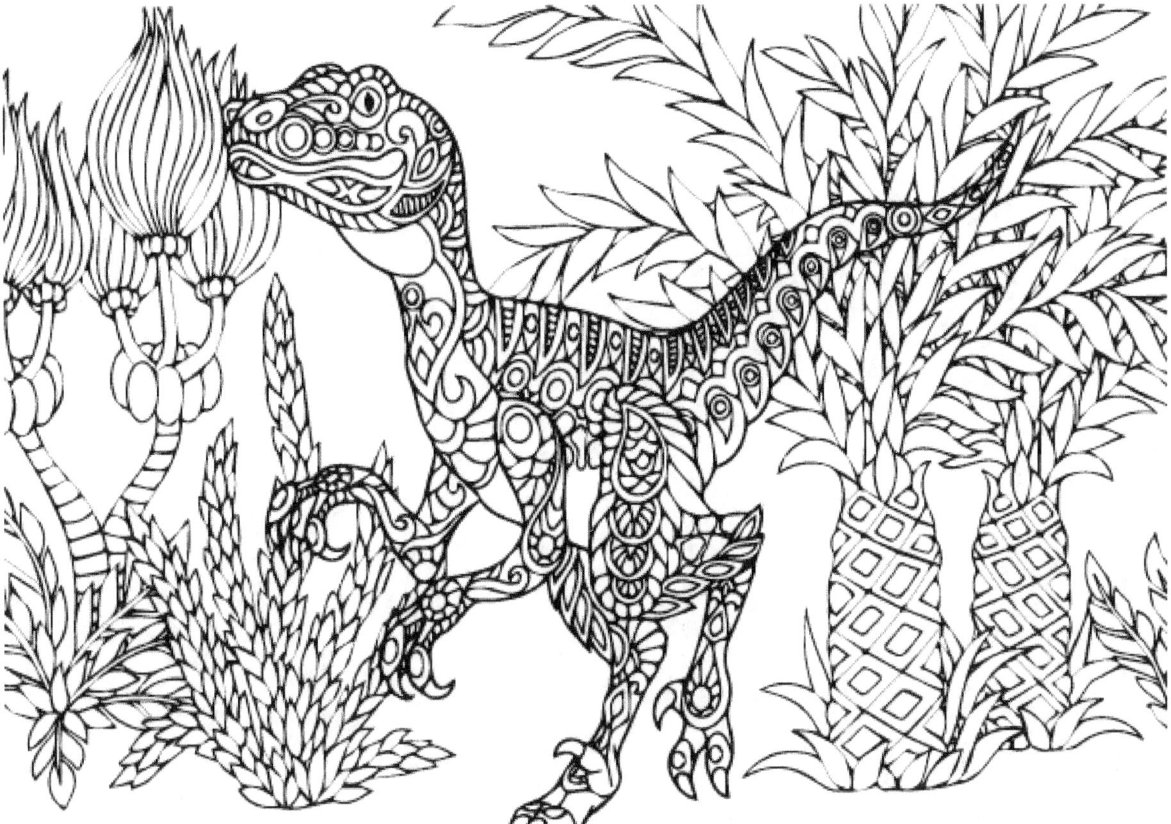

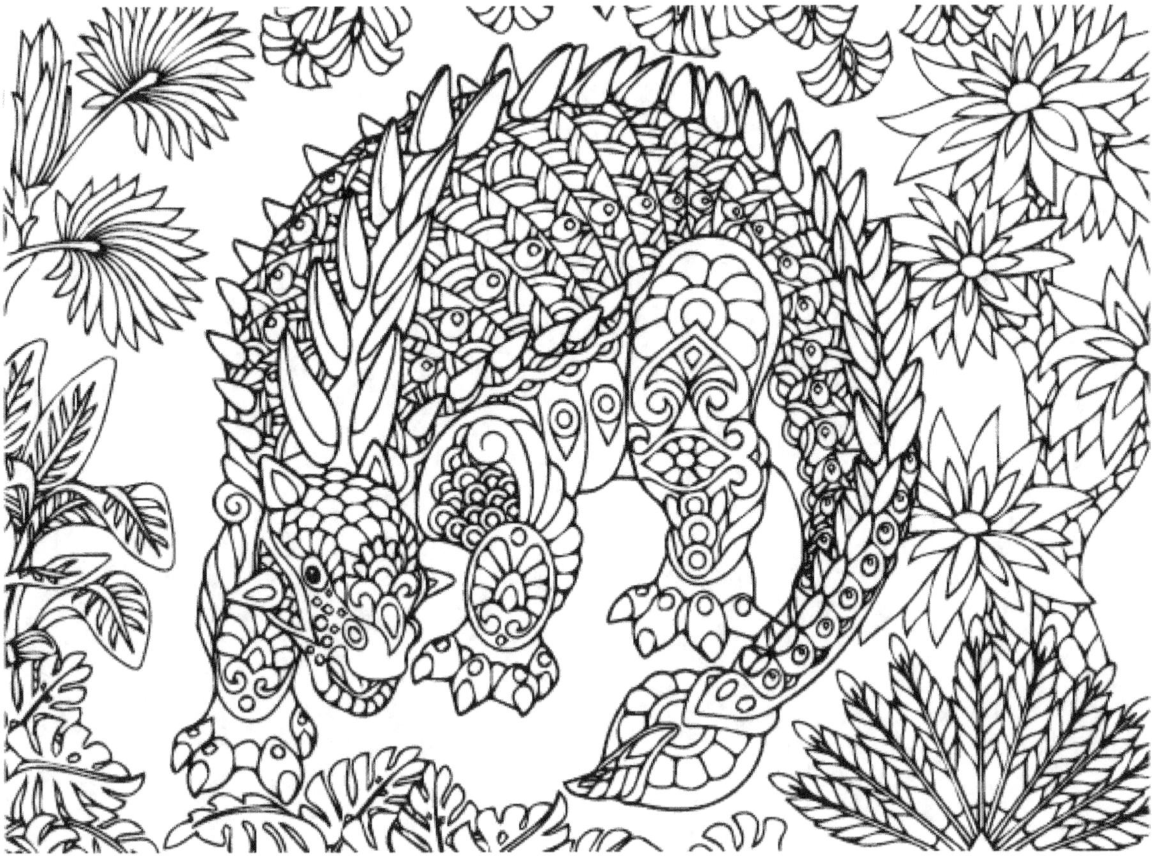

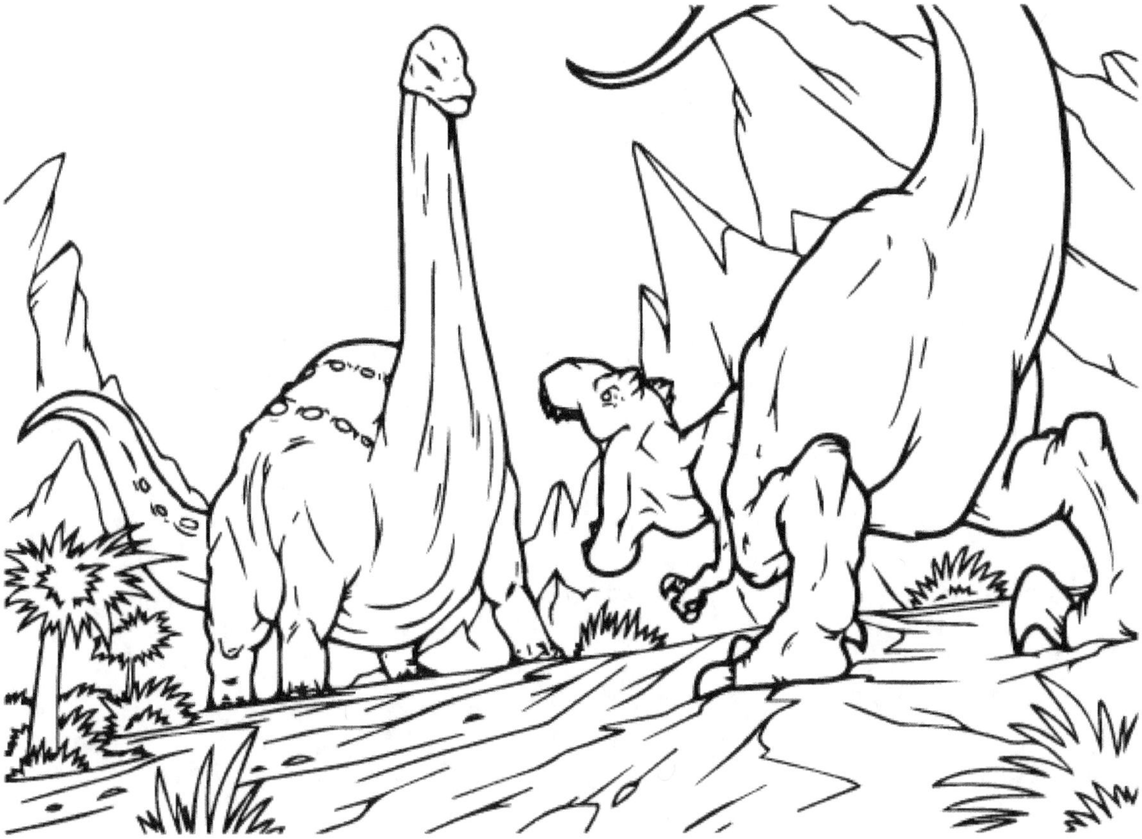

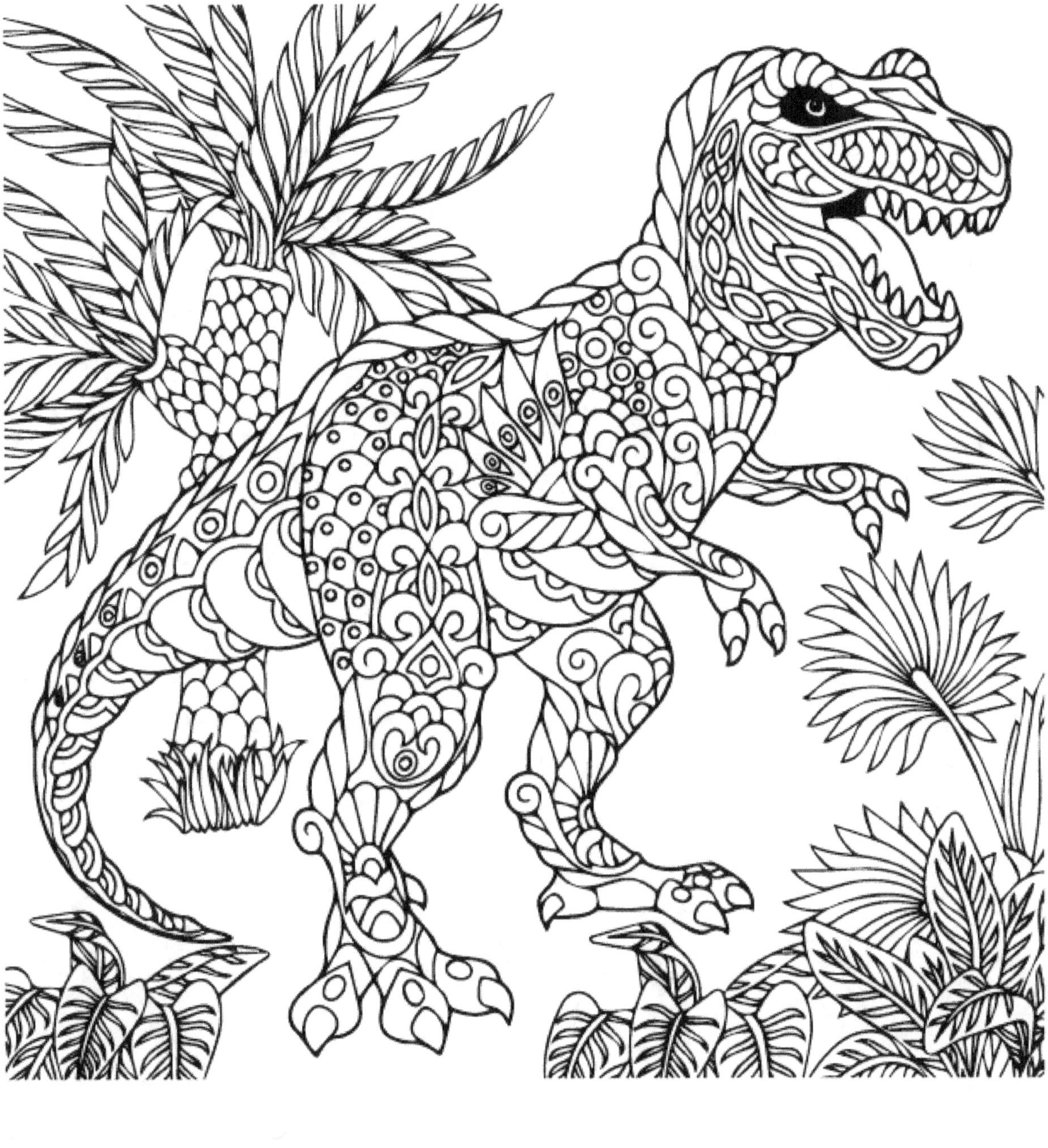

Dinosaur

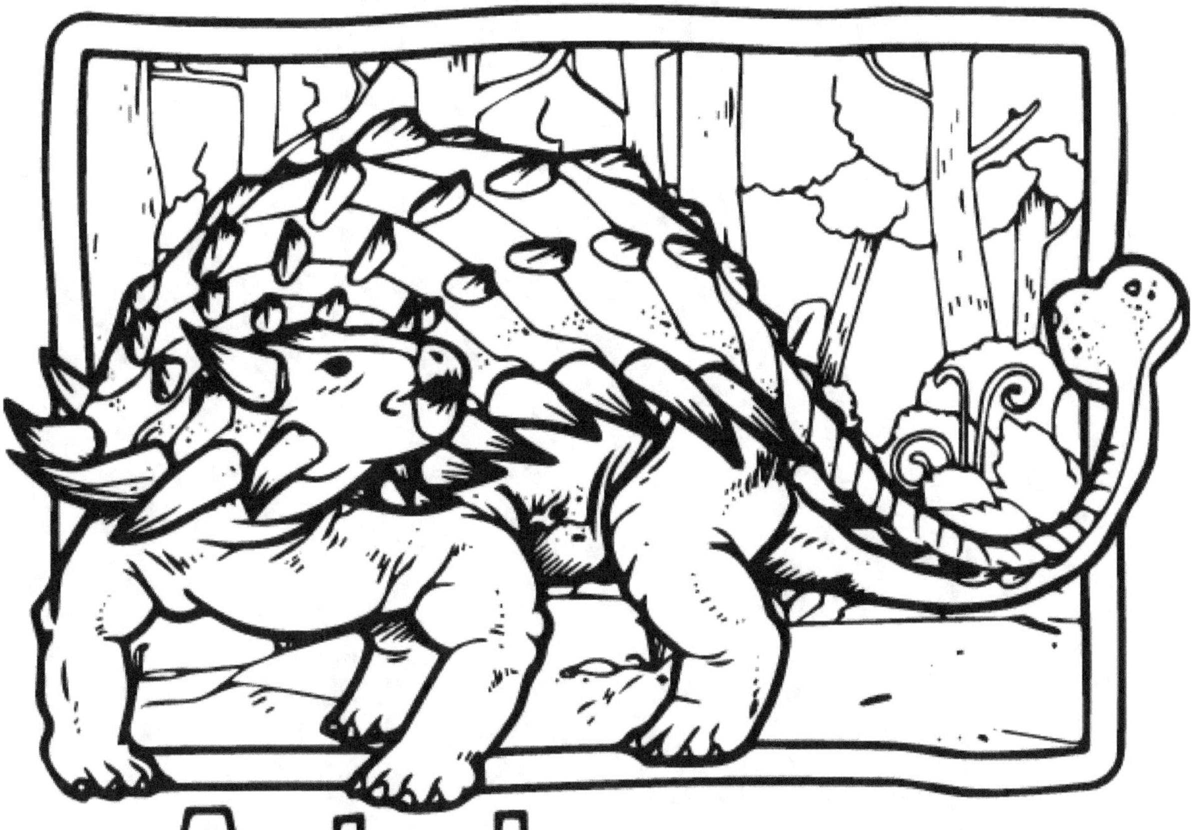

Ankylosaurus

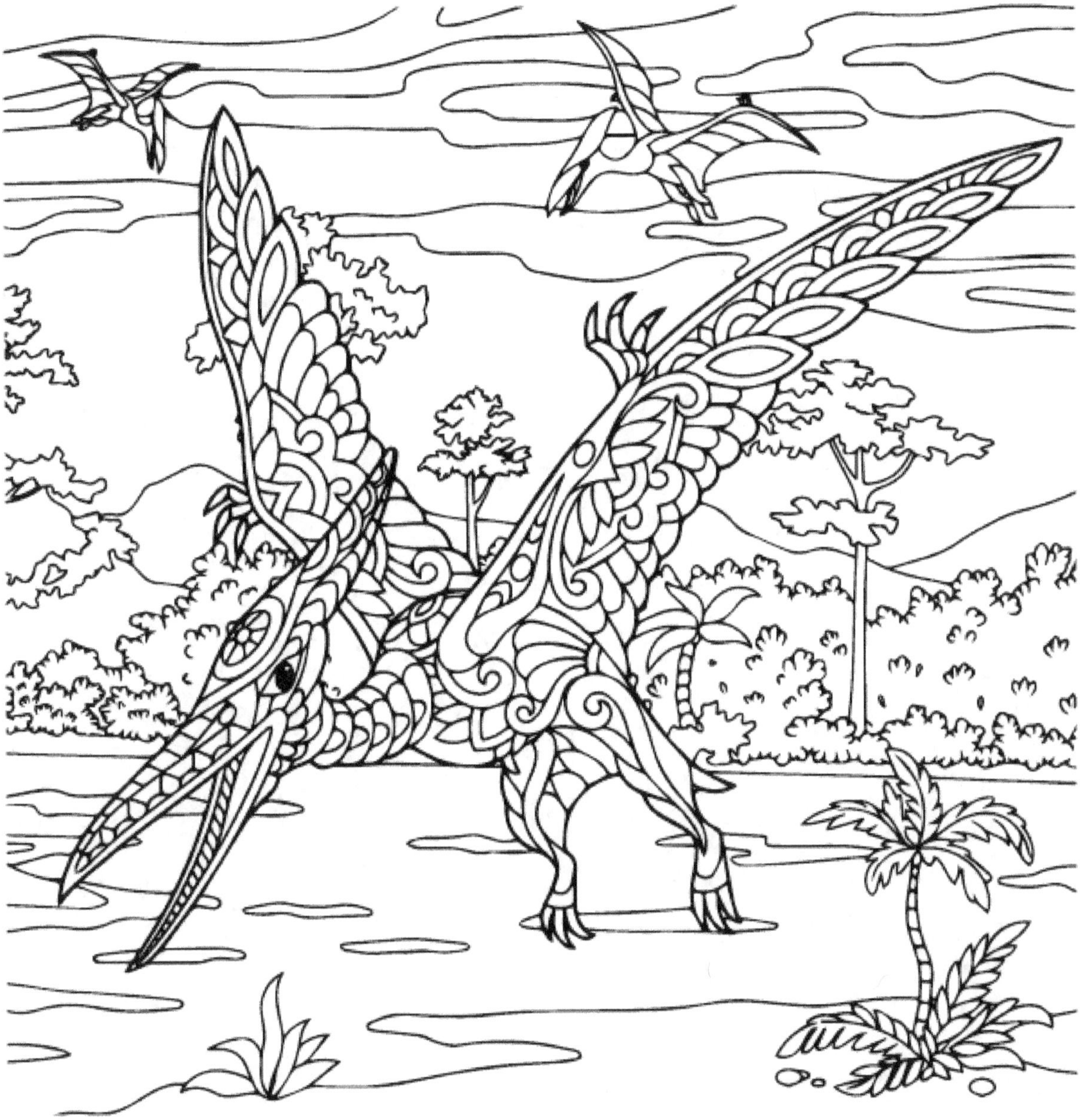

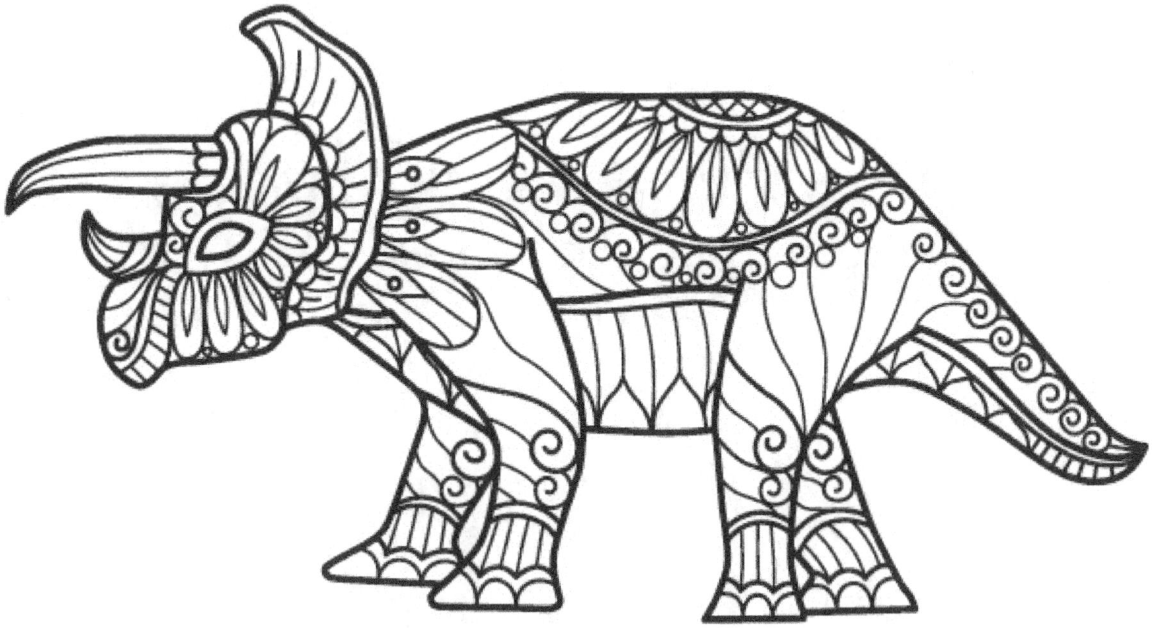

Dinosaur

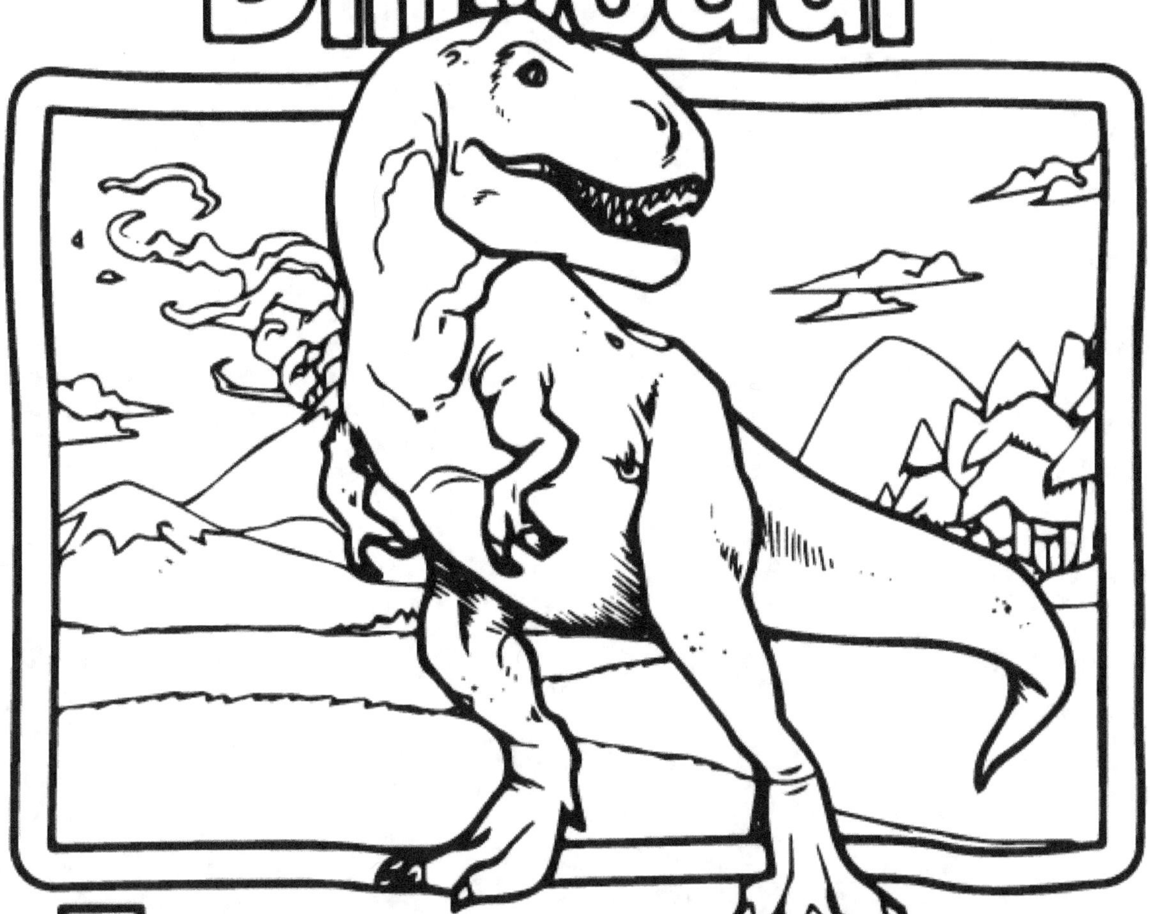

Tyrannosaurus

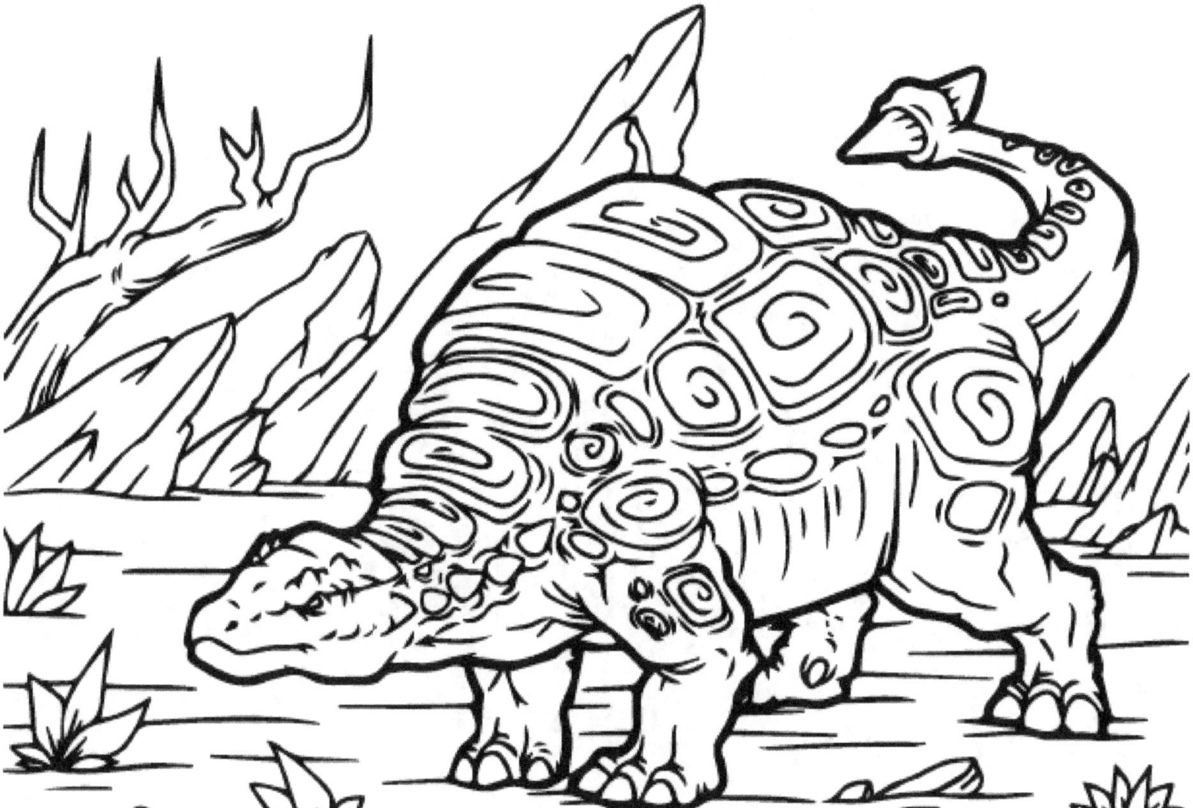

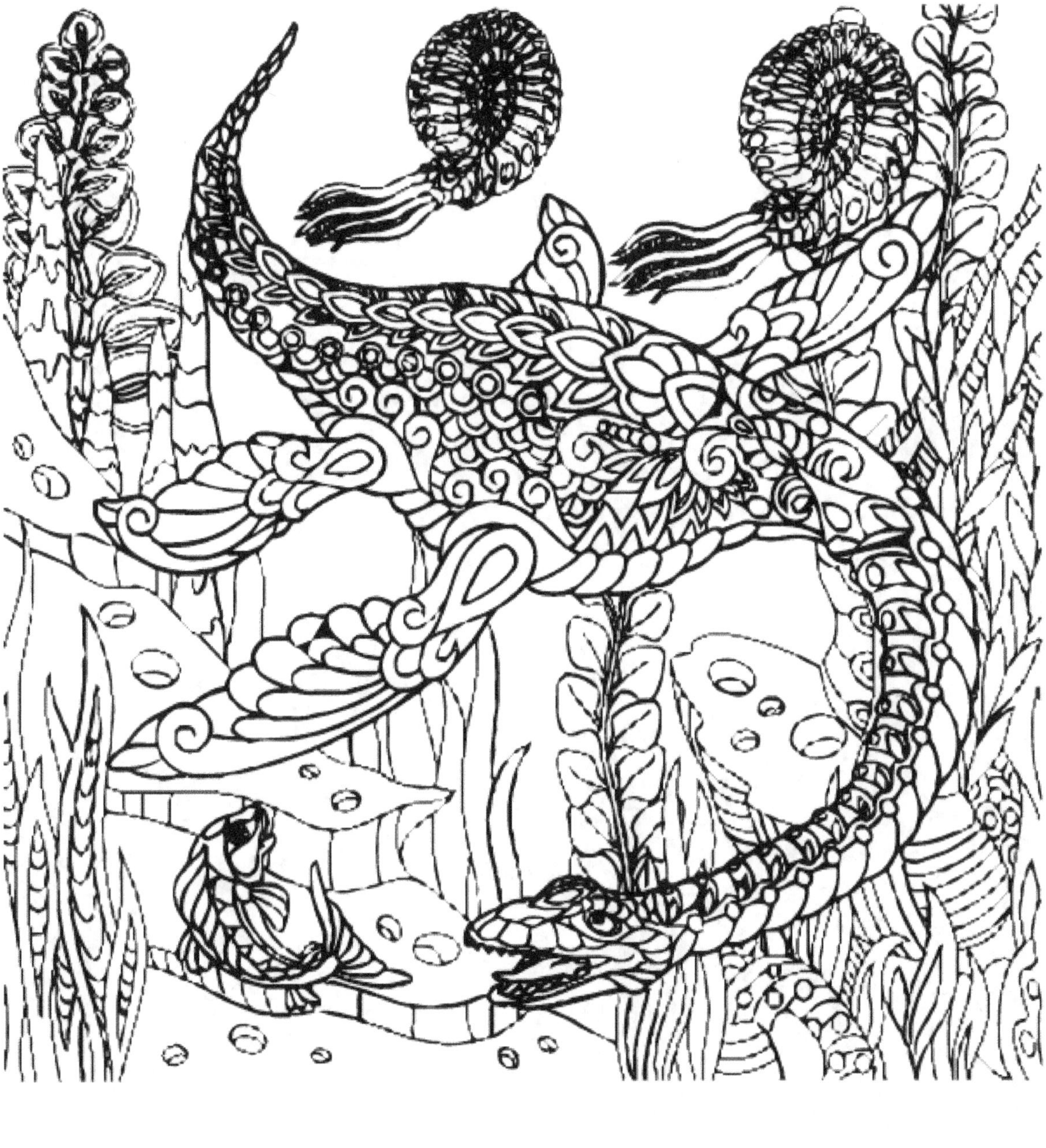

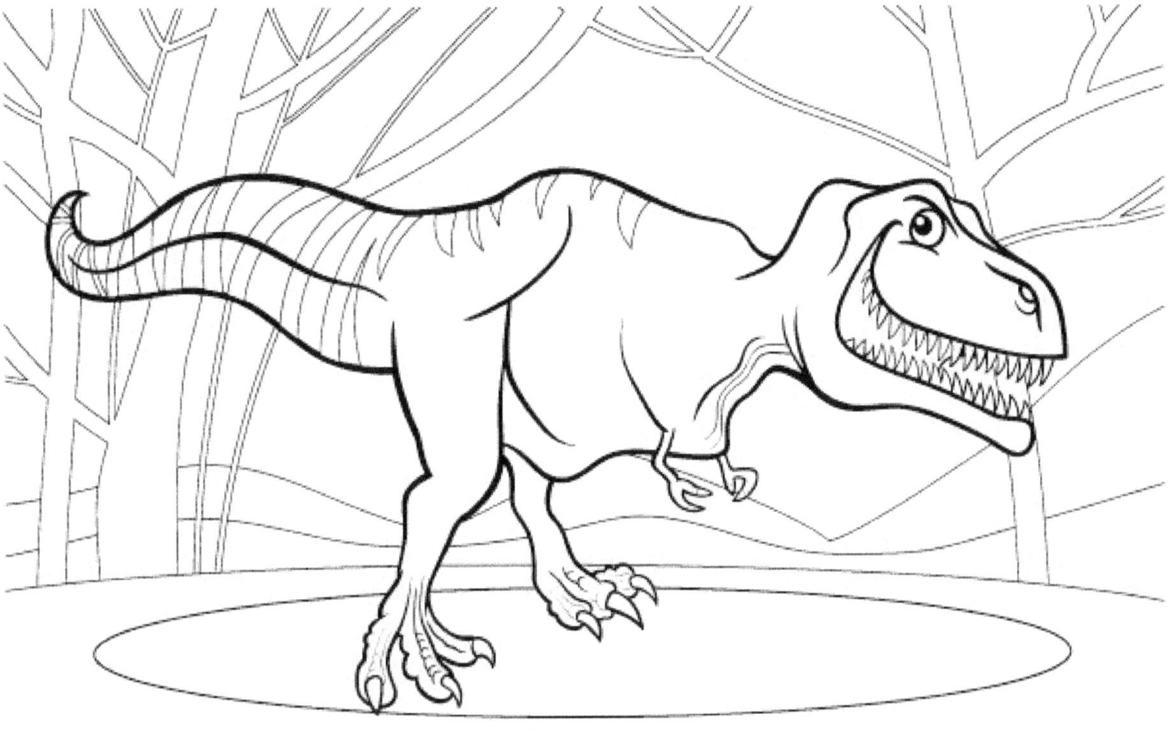

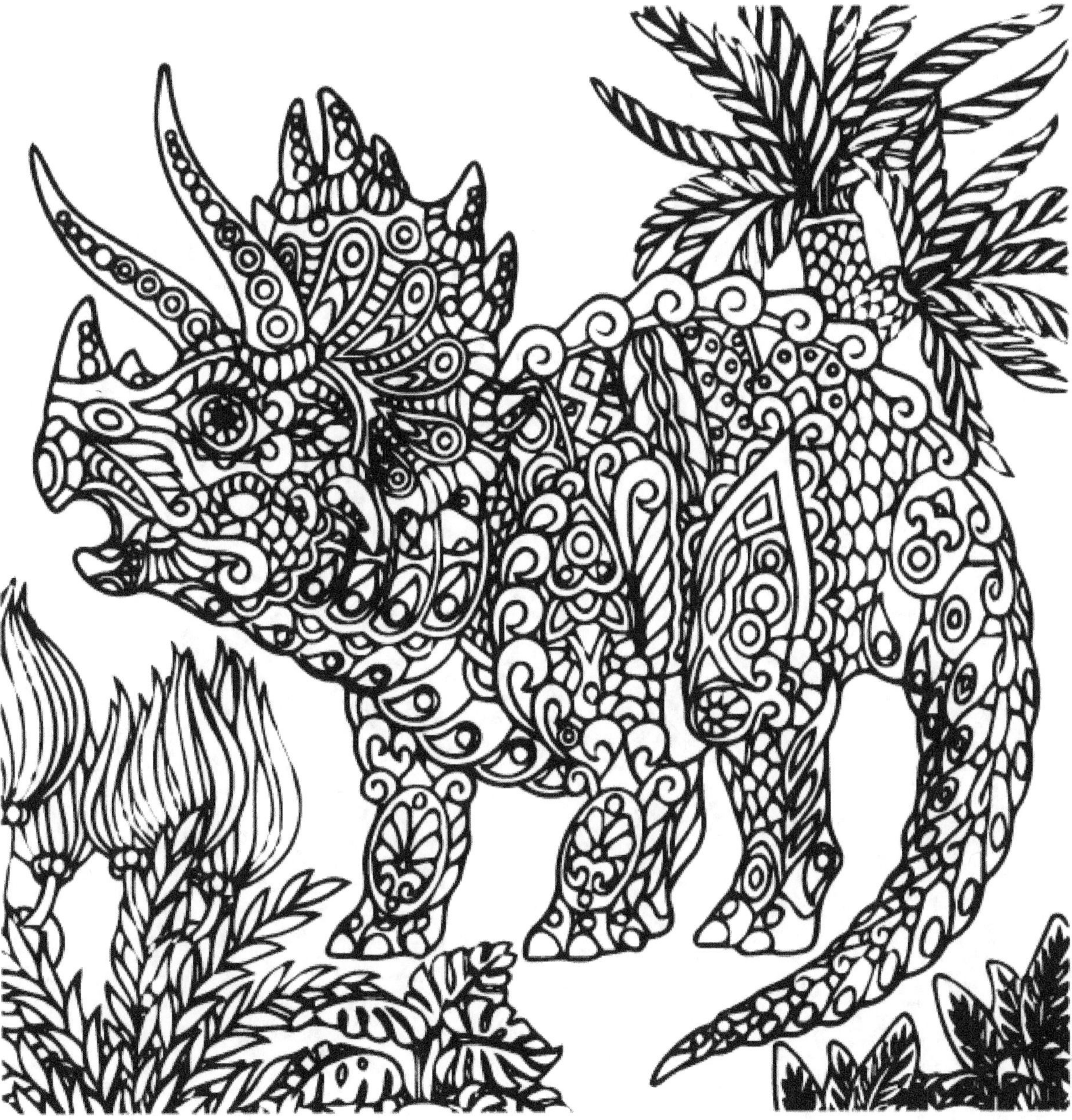

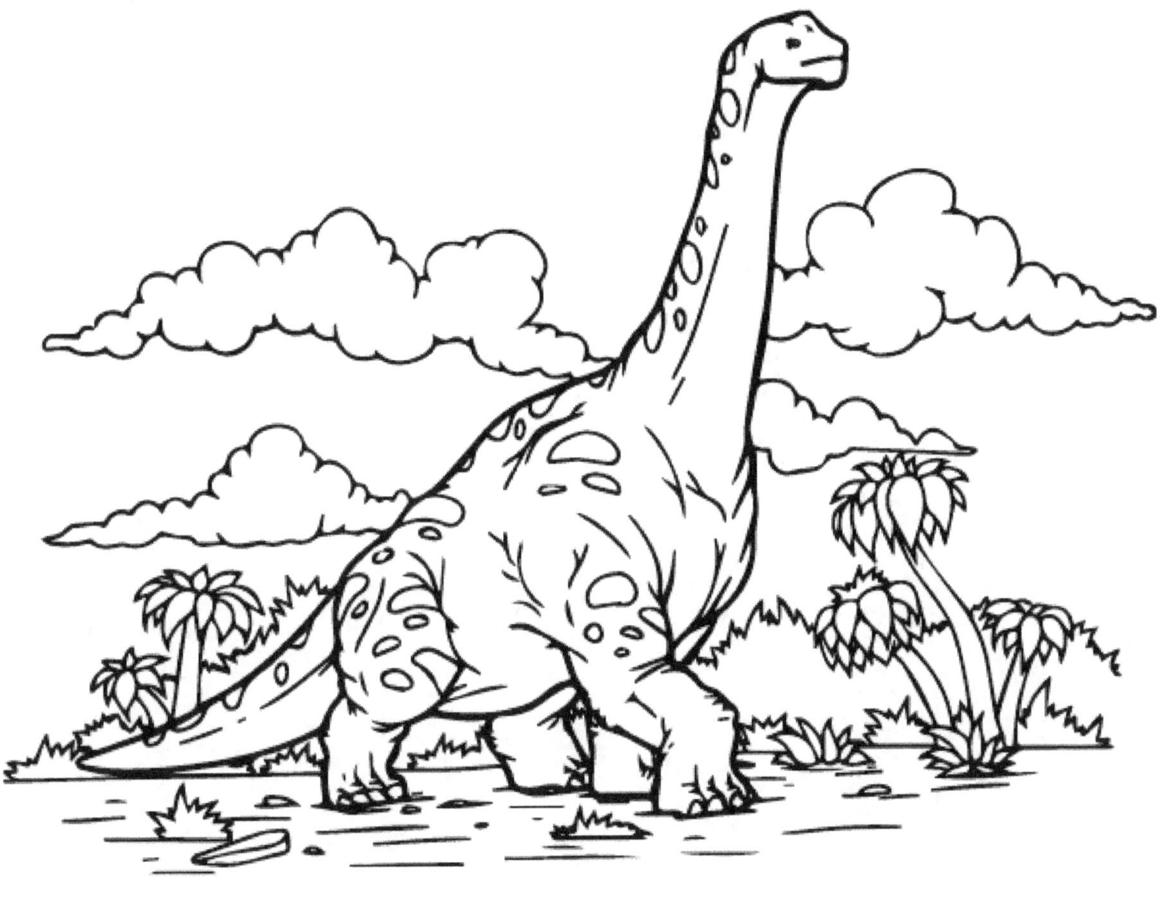

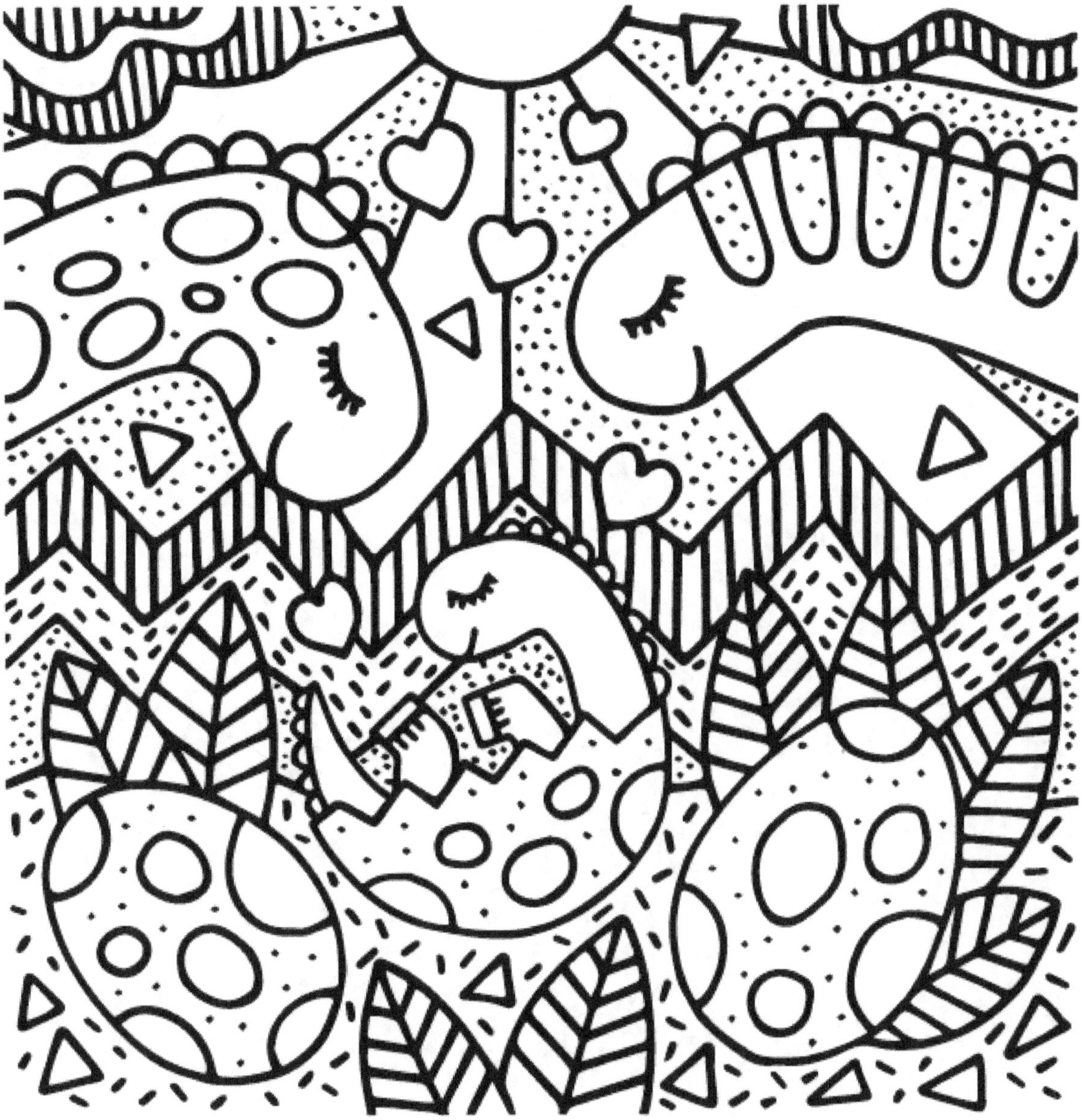

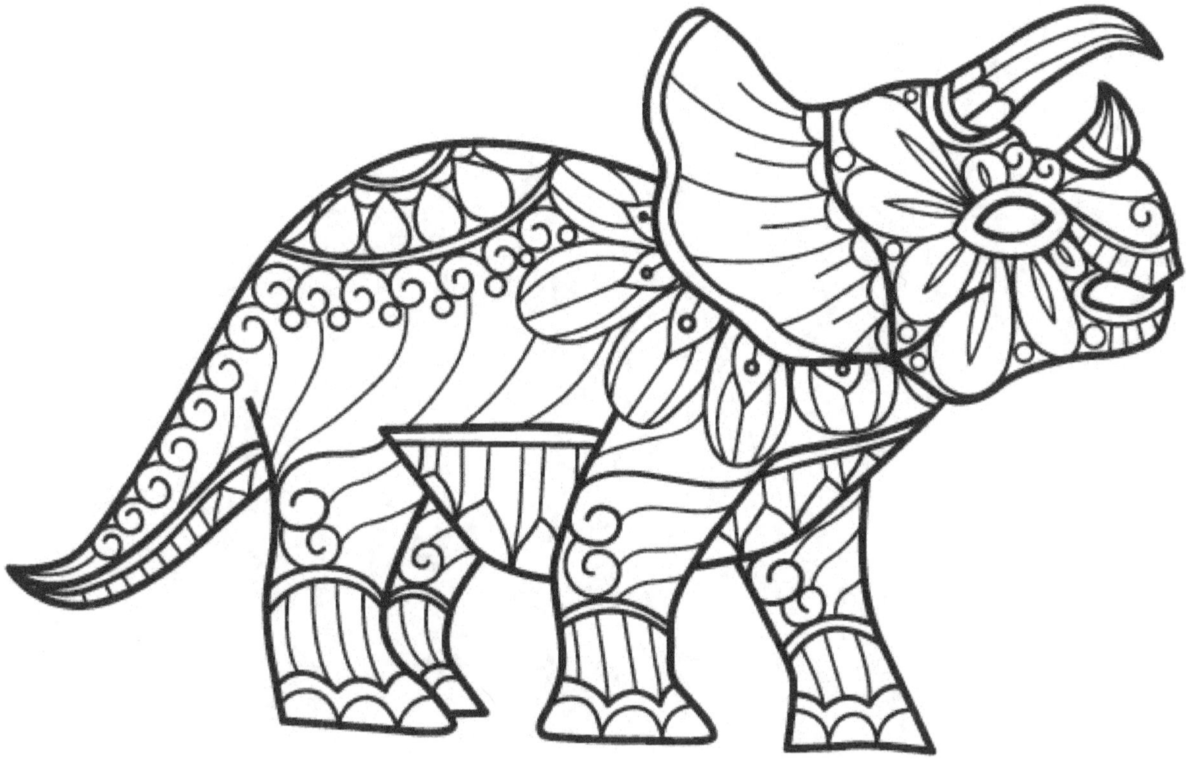

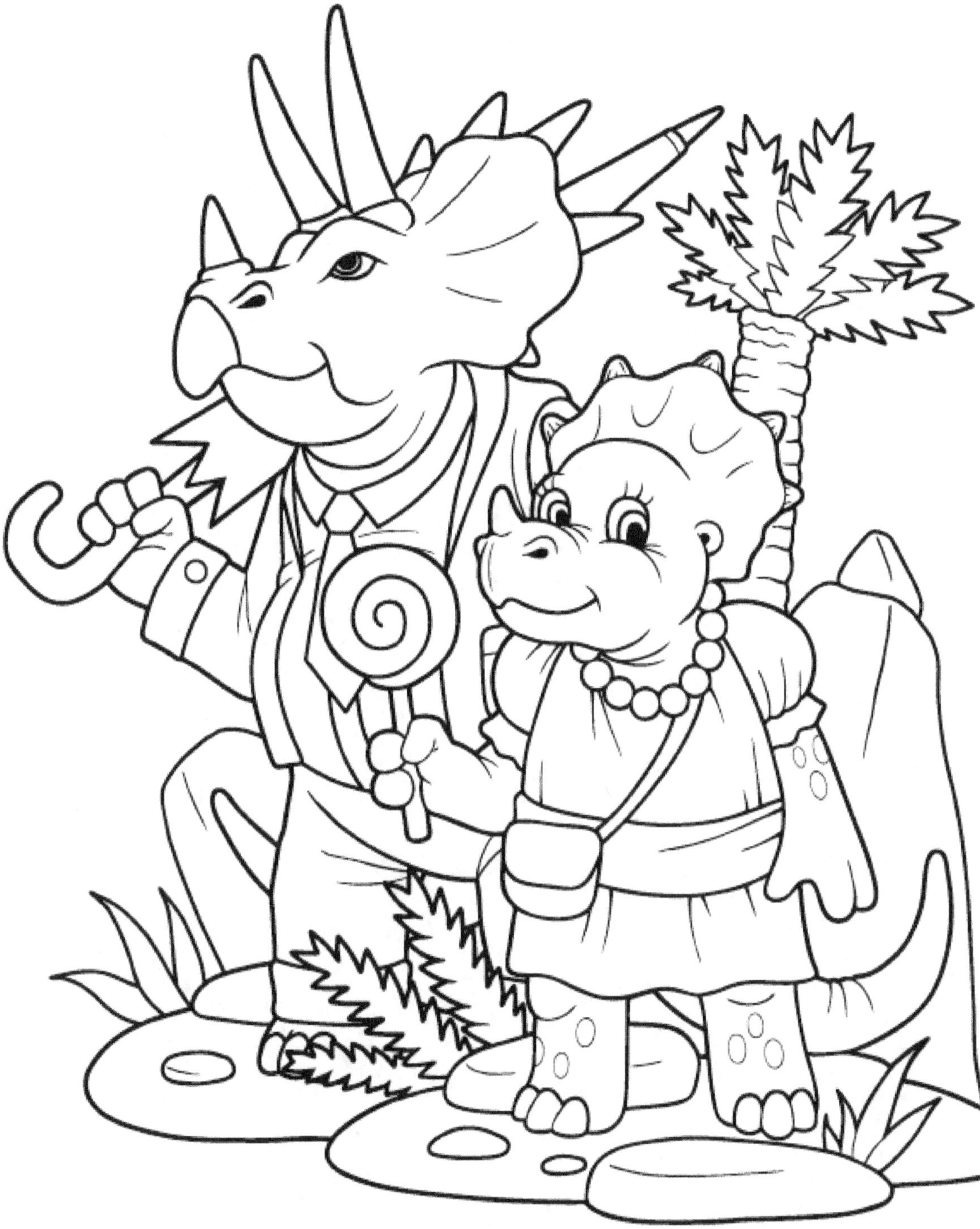

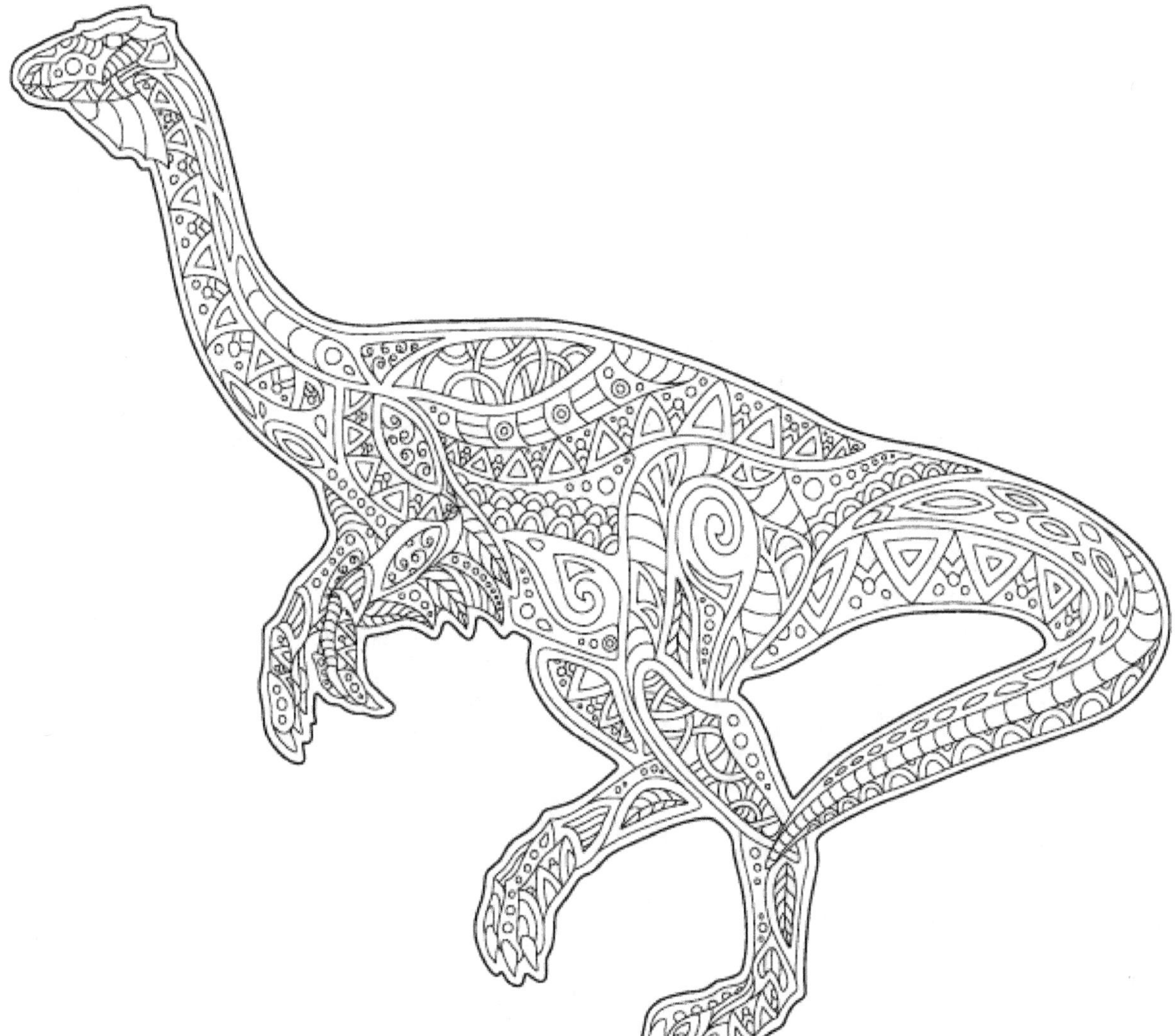

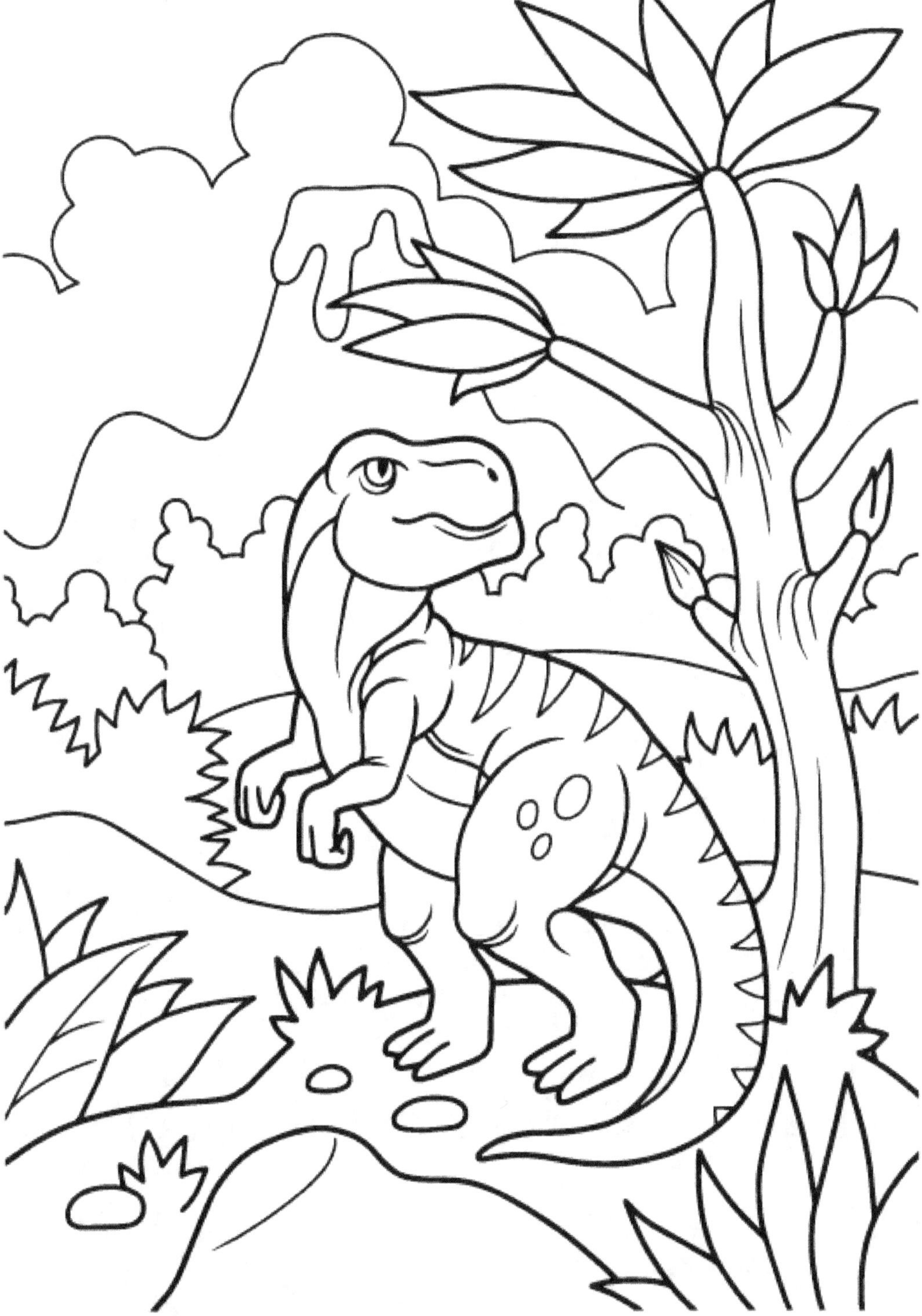

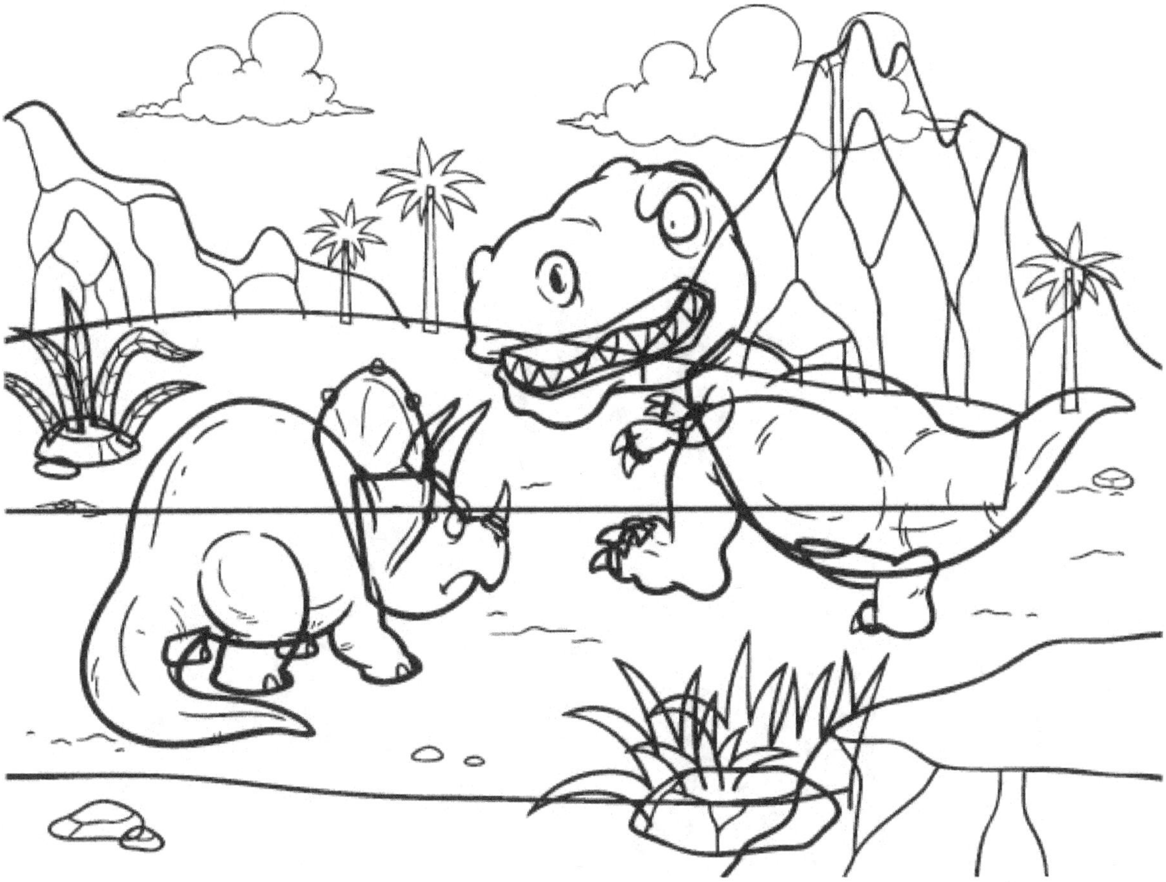

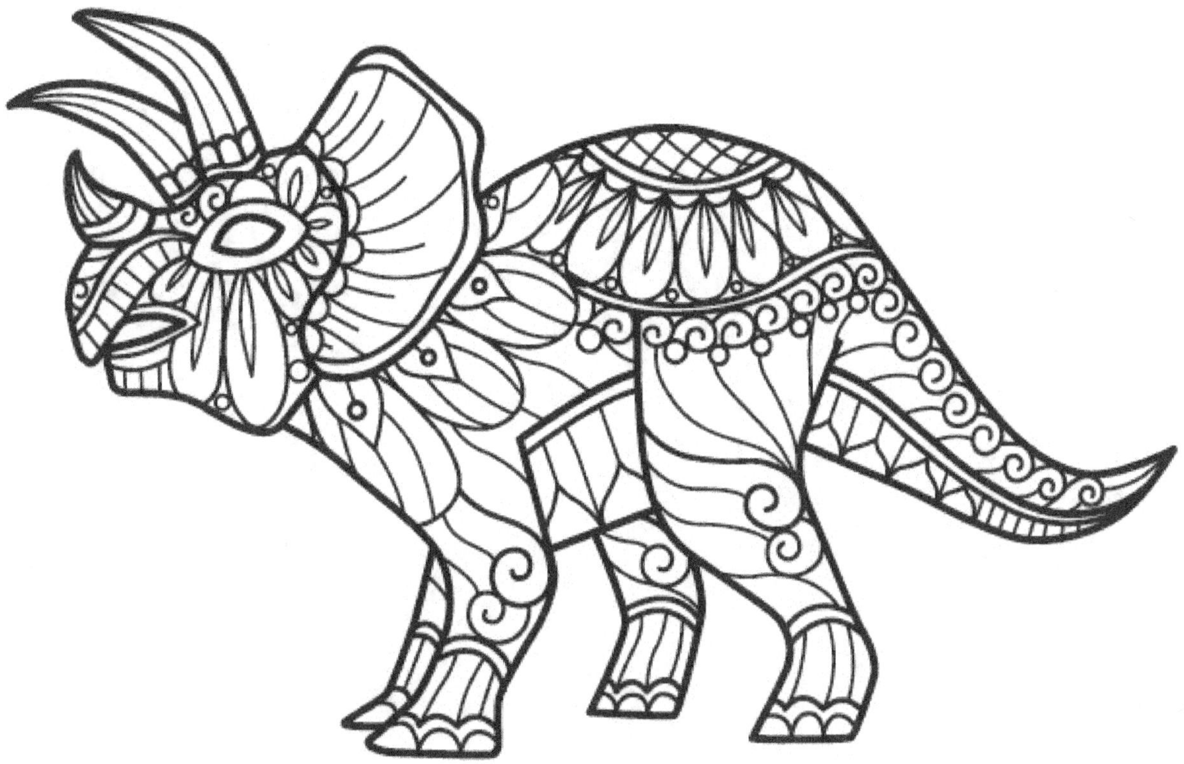

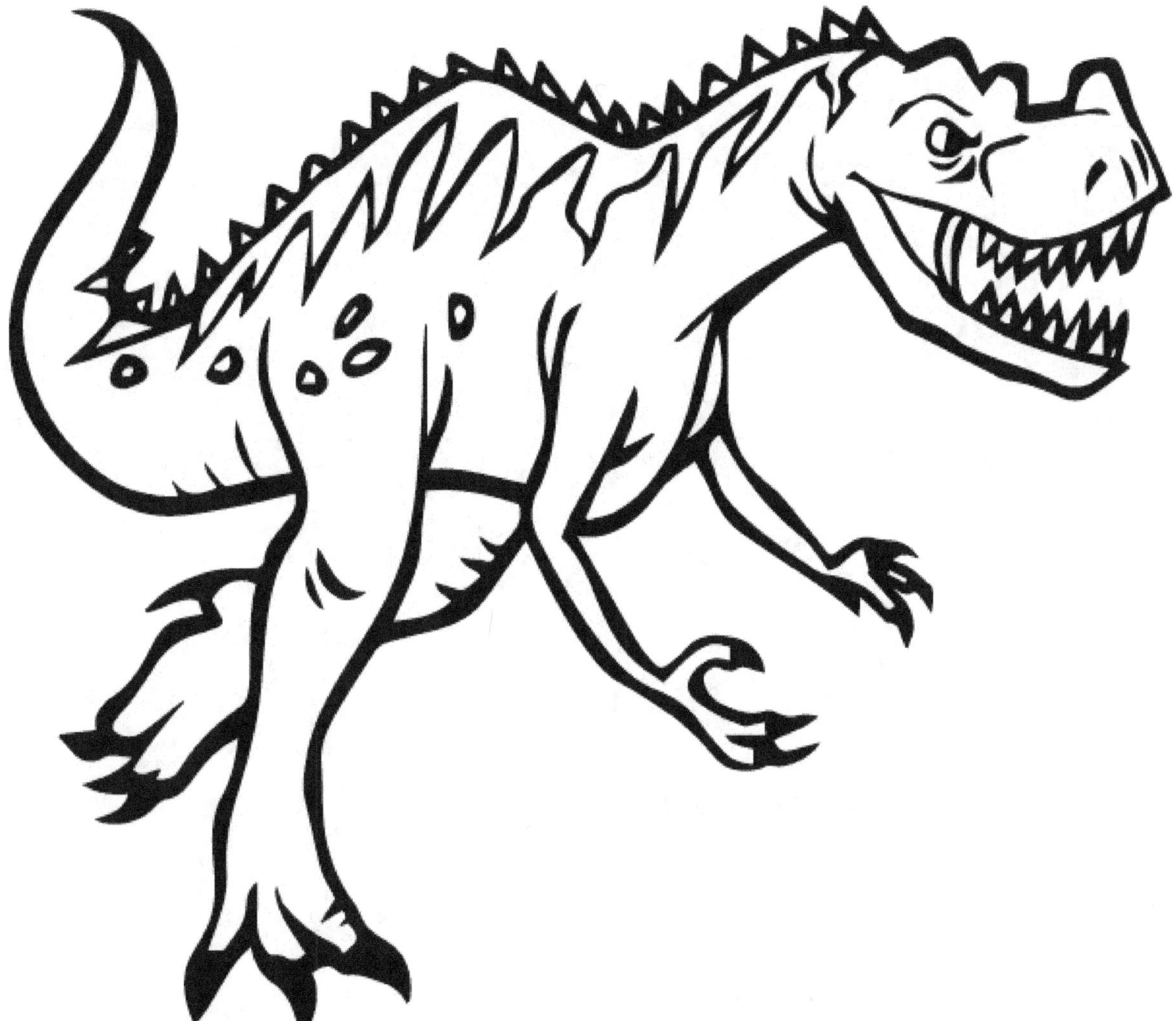

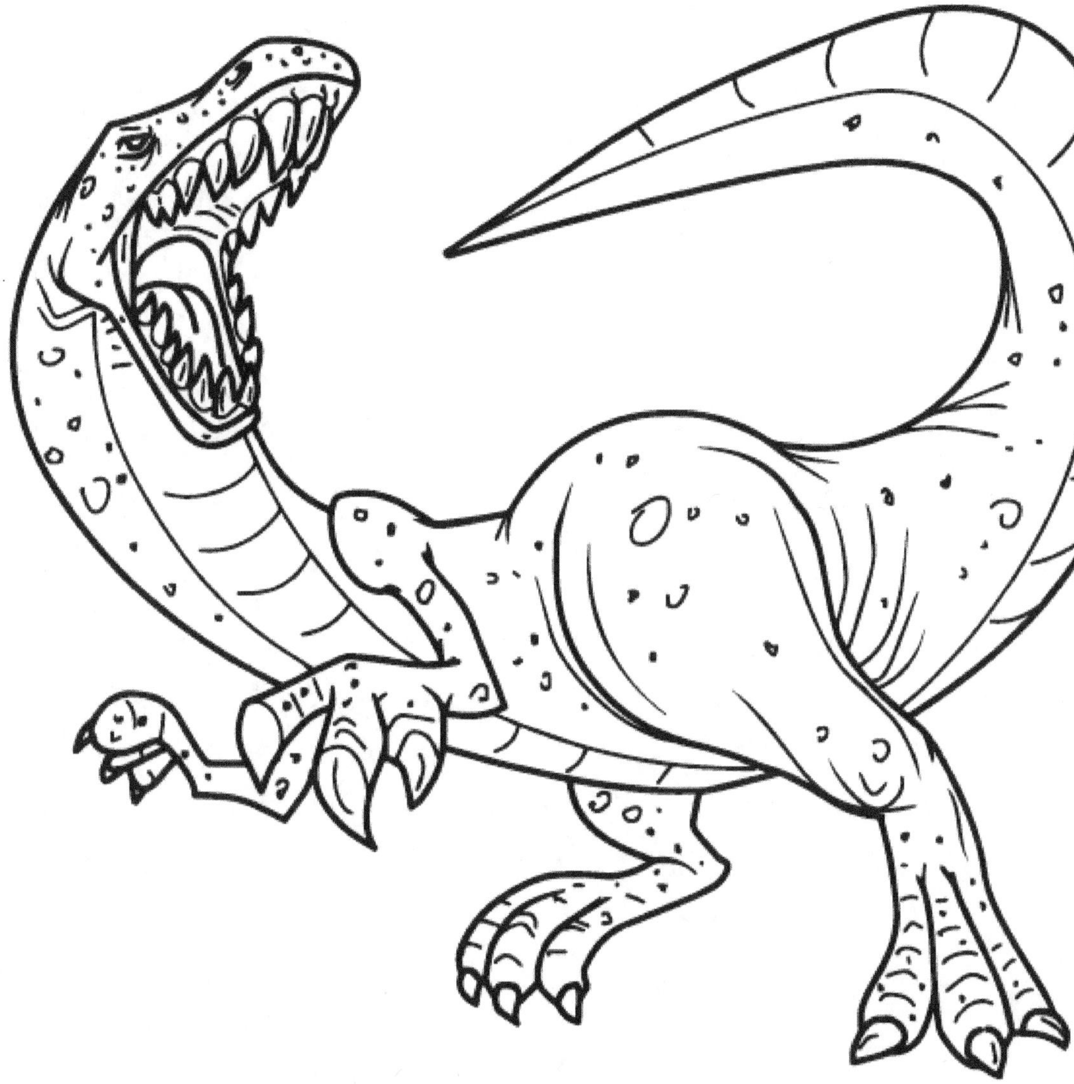

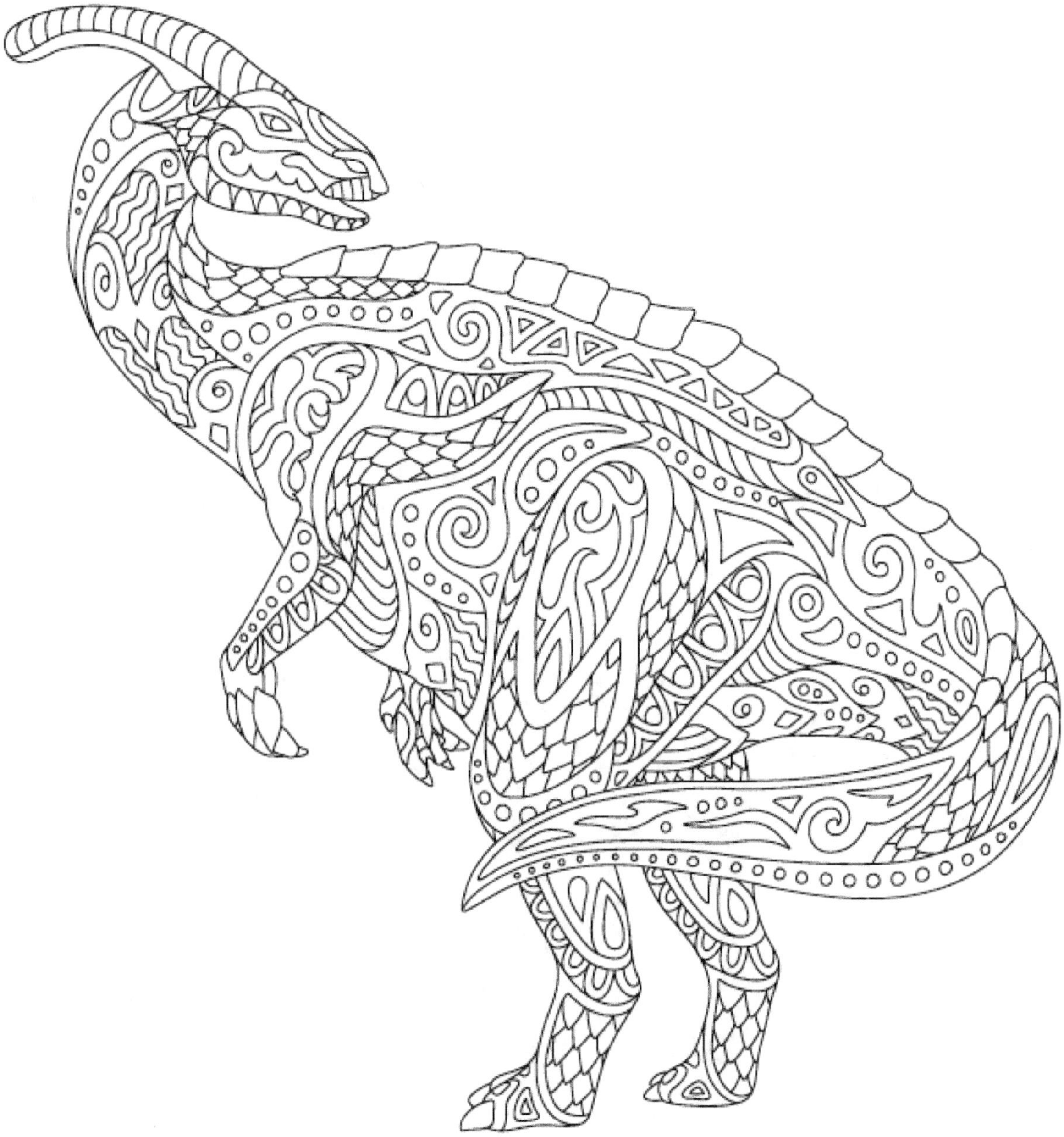

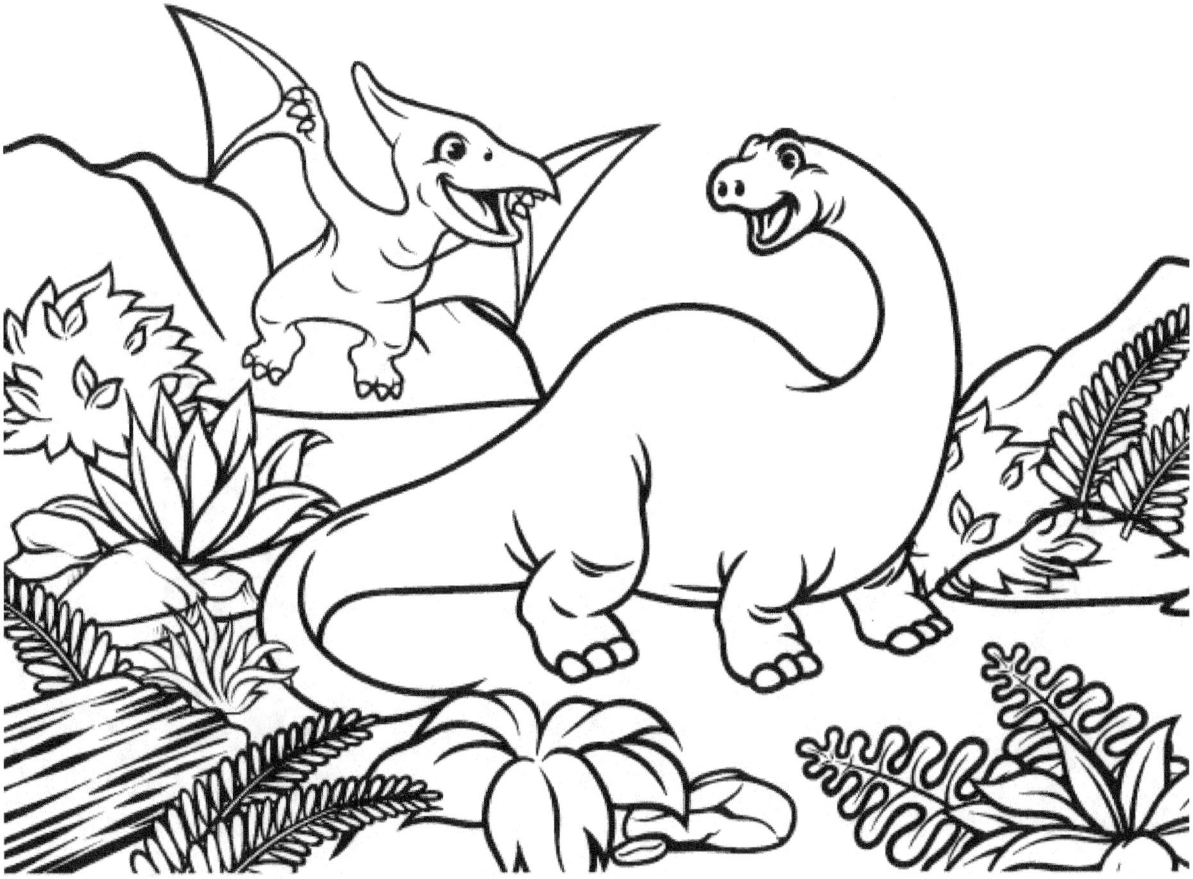

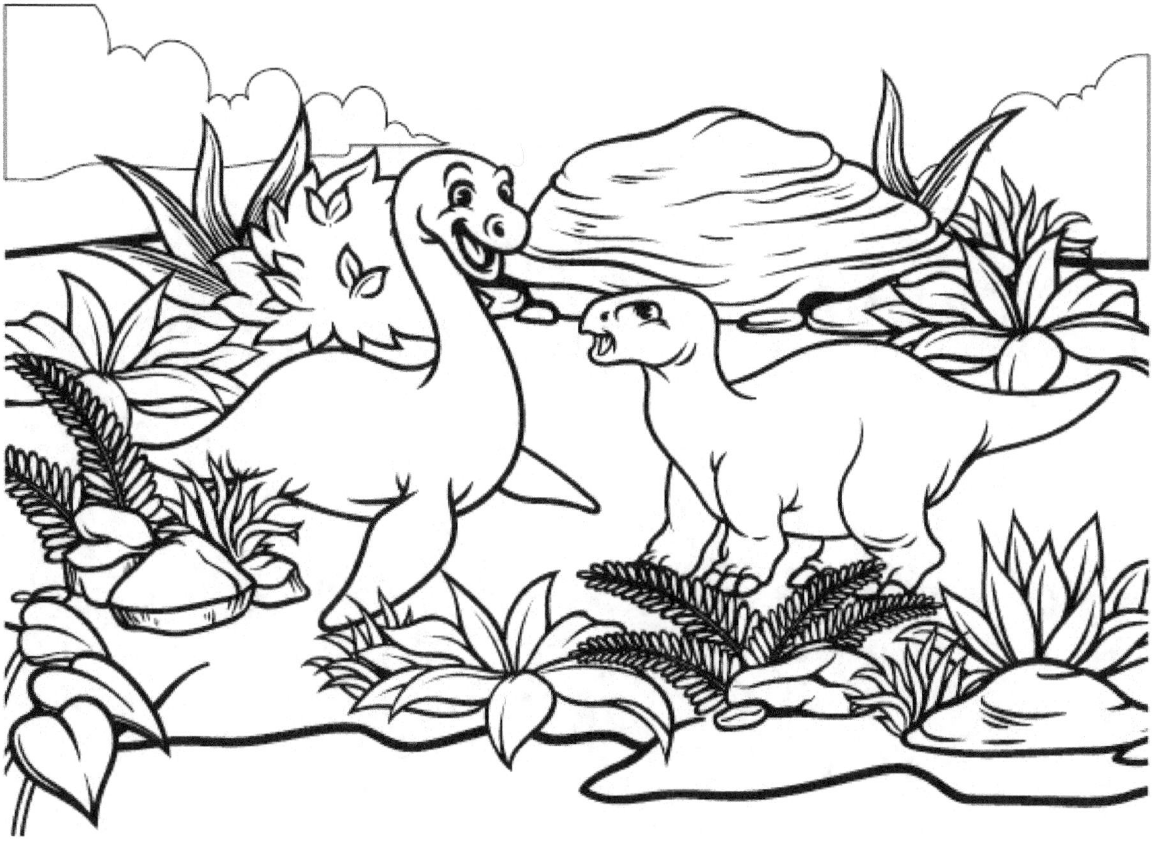

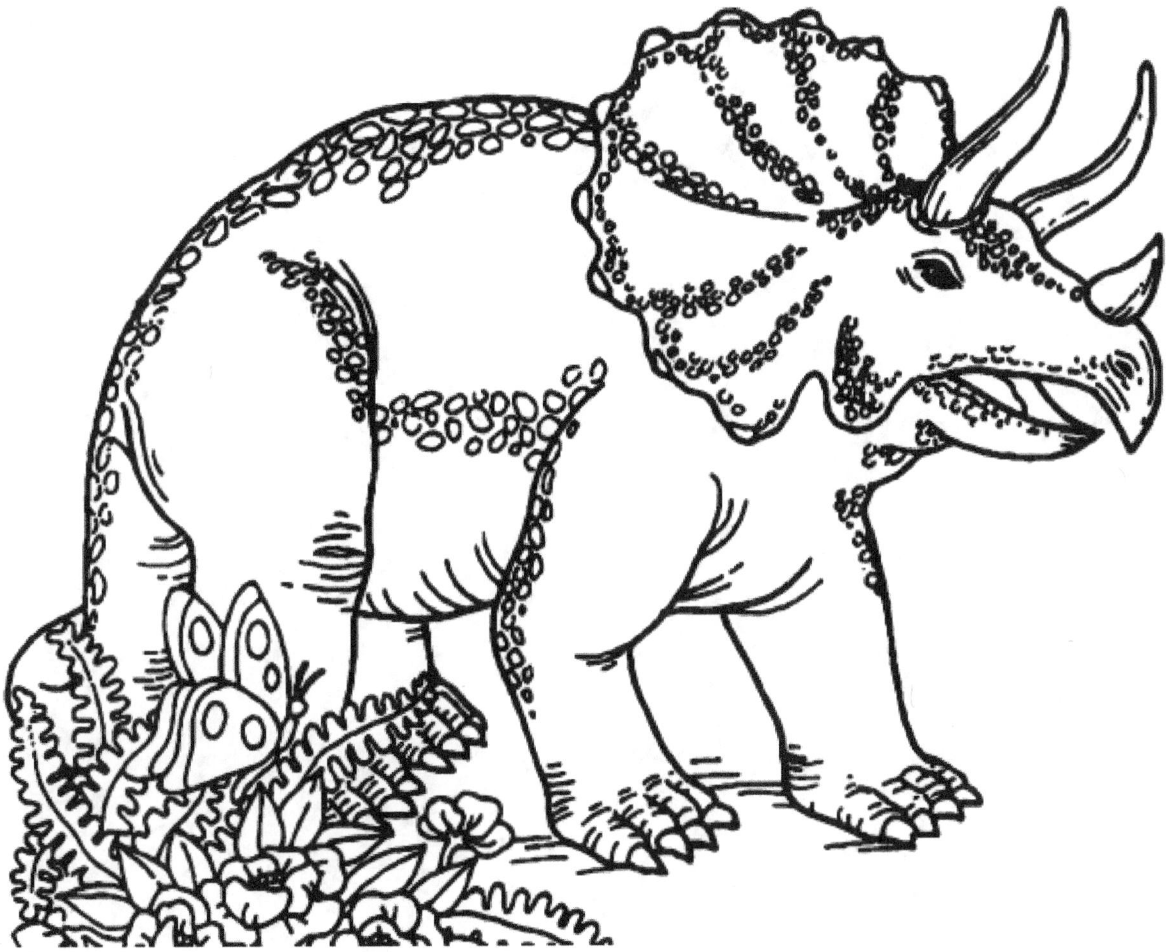

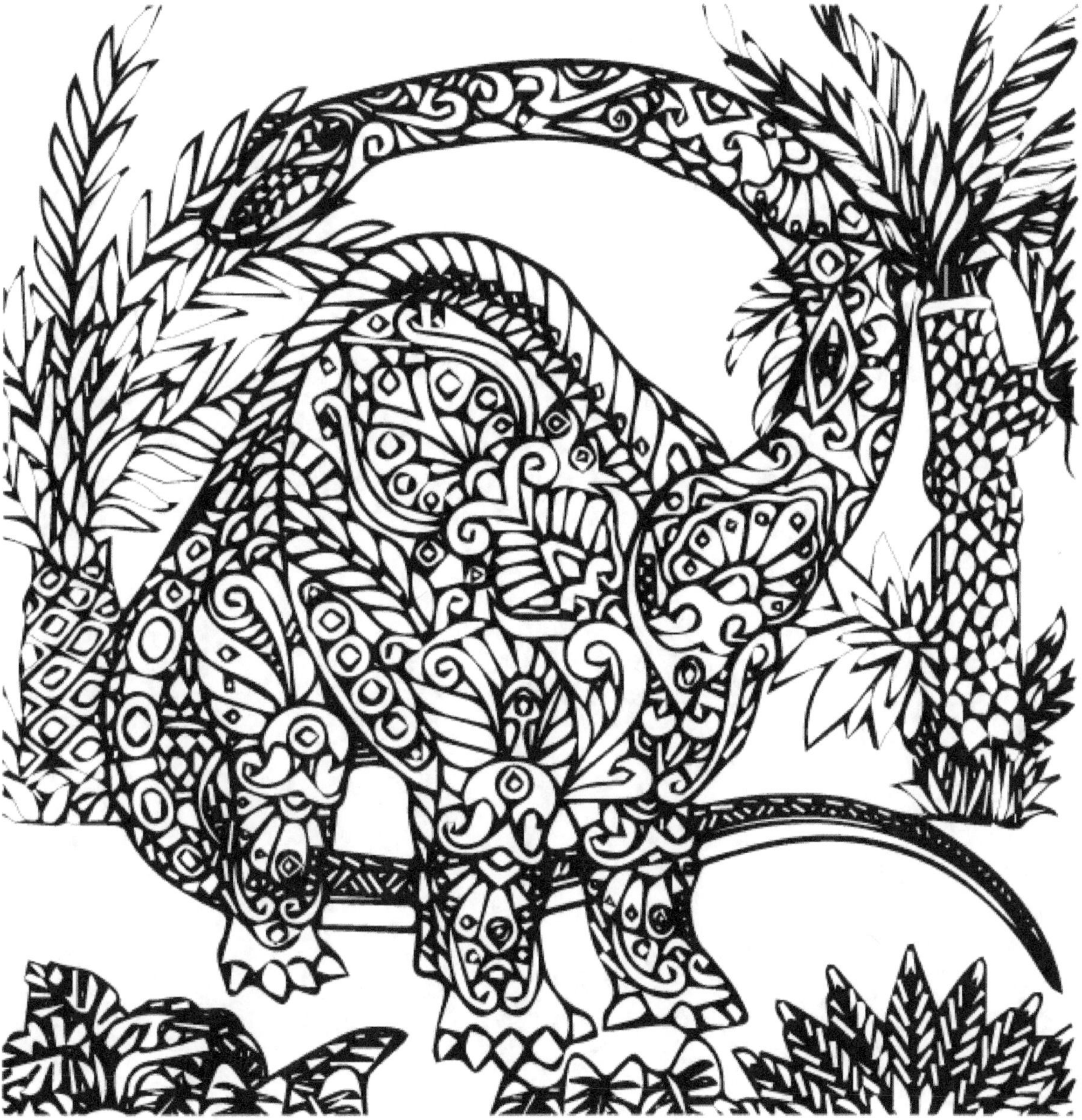

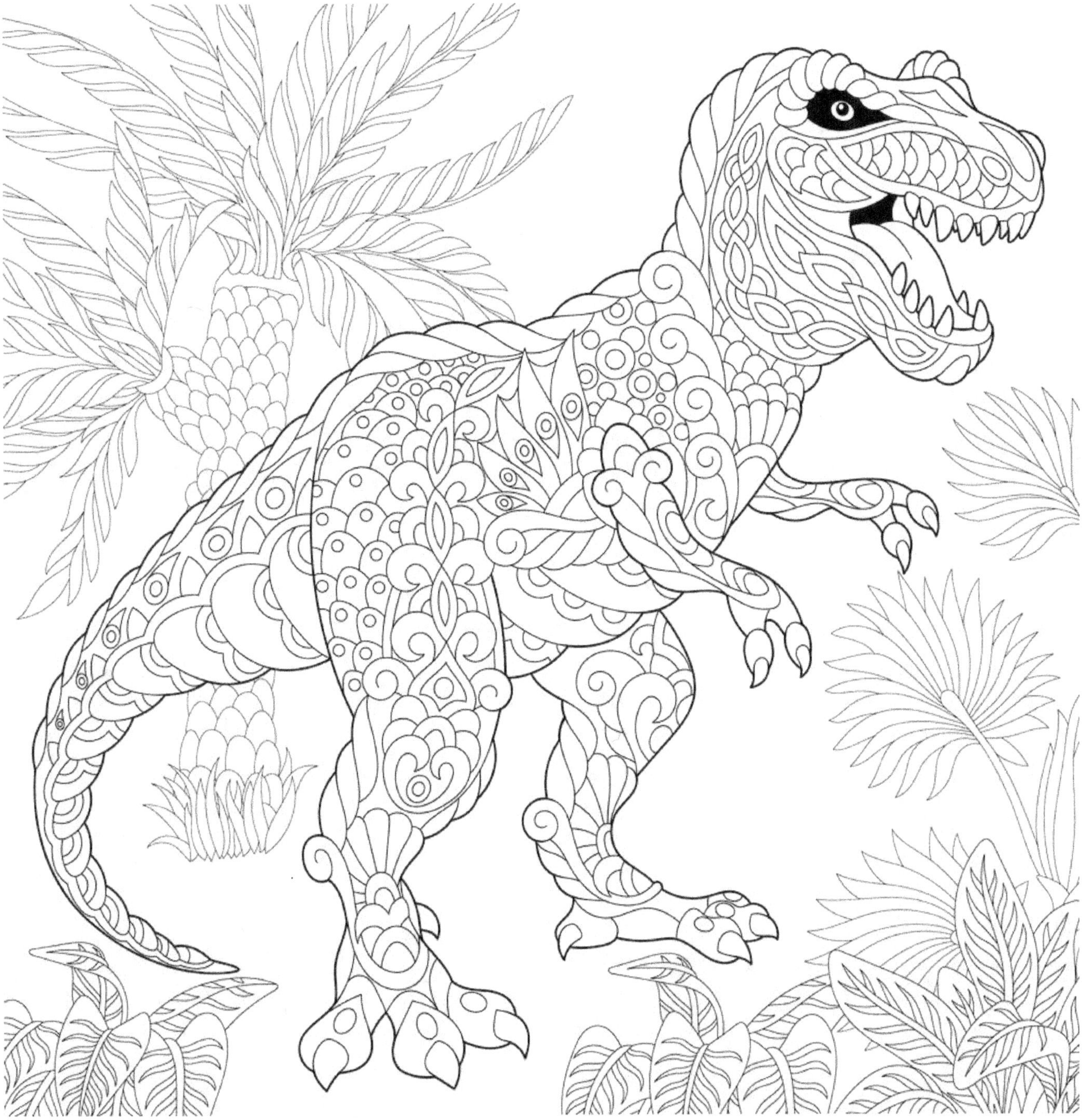

www.ingramcontent.com/pod-product-compliance
Lightning Source LLC
Chambersburg PA
CBHW082153230526
45467CB00044B/3200
* 9 7 9 8 6 8 7 3 0 5 4 5 7 *